Lecture Notes in Computer Science 16205

Founding Editors

Gerhard Goos
Juris Hartmanis

Editorial Board Members

The series Lecture Notes in Computer Science (LNCS), including its subseries Lecture Notes in Artificial Intelligence (LNAI) and Lecture Notes in Bioinformatics (LNBI), has established itself as a medium for the publication of new developments in computer science and information technology research, teaching, and education.

LNCS enjoys close cooperation with the computer science R & D community, the series counts many renowned academics among its volume editors and paper authors, and collaborates with prestigious societies. Its mission is to serve this international community by providing an invaluable service, mainly focused on the publication of conference and workshop proceedings and postproceedings. LNCS commenced publication in 1973.

Maxime Chamberland · Yuqian Chen ·
Patryk Filipiak · Tom Hendriks · Jinglei Lv ·
S. Shailja · Elinor Thompson
Editors

Computational Diffusion MRI

16th International Workshop, CDMRI 2025
Held in Conjunction with MICCAI 2025
Daejeon, South Korea, September 27, 2025
Proceedings

 Springer

Editors
Maxime Chamberland (iD)
Eindhoven University of Technology
Eindhoven, The Netherlands

Yuqian Chen
Harvard Medical School
Boston, MA, USA

Patryk Filipiak (iD)
NYU Langone Health
New York, NY, USA

Tom Hendriks (iD)
Eindhoven University of Technology
Eindhoven, The Netherlands

Jinglei Lv (iD)
University of Sydney
Sydney, NSW, Australia

S. Shailja (iD)
Stanford University
Palo Alto, CA, USA

Elinor Thompson (iD)
University College London
London, UK

ISSN 0302-9743   ISSN 1611-3349 (electronic)
Lecture Notes in Computer Science
ISBN 978-3-032-12836-2   ISBN 978-3-032-12837-9 (eBook)
https://doi.org/10.1007/978-3-032-12837-9

Preface

We are excited to share the proceedings of the 2025 Computational Diffusion MRI (CDMRI) workshop. For over ten years, this workshop has been a key satellite event at the Medical Image Computing and Computer Assisted Intervention (MICCAI) conference. This year, CDMRI once again served as a stage to highlight some of the freshest breakthroughs in diffusion MRI research at MICCAI in Daejeon, South Korea.

Diffusion-weighted imaging, or diffusion MRI, offers a unique, non-invasive window into the microstructure of biological tissue. Over the last forty years, the field has seen remarkable progress in how we acquire, analyze, and apply diffusion MRI, bringing us closer to reliable clinical tools that can detect subtle tissue changes in the brain and beyond. It remains the only method capable of mapping the brain's white matter pathways in living subjects, with brain tractography techniques steadily improving. But despite all this progress, diffusion MRI still faces significant challenges: from making the technology more accessible and clinically practical, to extending its use beyond the brain, and tackling the ongoing variability in tractography methods that complicates clinical adoption. The contributions to CDMRI 2025 presented innovative approaches addressing these critical hurdles, pushing the community forward.

This year's CDMRI workshop featured two keynote lectures by our invited speakers and eight long oral presentations. The first keynote, delivered by Susie Y. Huang was especially fitting for South Korea, a global leader of technology development. Huang's lecture focused on developing, validating, and translating high-gradient diffusion MRI for noninvasive measurements of axonal integrity and early neurodegeneration in multiple sclerosis and aging. The second keynote, delivered by Jelle Veraart, highlighted a global community benchmark for brain microstructure and connectivity processing pipelines. The central message of this lecture was that the lack of standardization and harmonization across software pipelines remains the dominant source of variability in diffusion MRI metrics of brain microstructure and connectivity. Both keynote lectures were followed by lively discussions and extended Q/A sessions. The oral presentations covered a broad range of themes, from advances in white matter mapping (including streamline analysis, bundle segmentation, and biophysical microvascular modeling) to clinical applications of diffusion MRI (with emphasis on modeling and applications in brain pathology).

This workshop would not have been possible without the dedication of the Program Committee (listed below), who, through a double-blind peer review process, ensured the highest standard of submissions was achieved. Of the 10 submissions we received, 8 were accepted after revisions, and 2 were rejected; each submission was reviewed by at least three members of the Program Committee. We extend our gratitude to everyone involved in the Program Committee. Finally, we wish to thank our Keynote Speakers (listed below), who delivered a series of truly enlightening lectures.

September 2025

Maxime Chamberland
Yuqian Chen
Patryk Filipiak
Tom Hendriks
Jinglei Lv
S. Shailja
Elinor Thompson

Organization

Organisers

Maxime Chamberland	Eindhoven University of Technology, The Netherlands
Yuqian Chen	Harvard Medical School, USA
Patryk Filipiak	NYU Langone Health, USA
Tom Hendriks	Eindhoven University of Technology, The Netherlands
Jinglei Lv	University of Sydney, Australia
S. Shailja	Stanford University, USA
Elinor Thompson	University College London, UK

Program Committee

Alessandro Daducci	Università di Verona, Italy
Alonso Ramirez-Manzanares	CIMAT A.C., Mexico
Amy Howard	Imperial College London, UK
Andrey I. Zhylka	UMC Utrecht, The Netherlands
Anna Schroder	University College London, UK
Antoine Théberge	Université de Sherbrooke, Canada
Christophe Lenglet	University of Minnesota, USA
Daniel C. Moyer	Vanderbilt University, USA
Fang-cheng Yeh	University of Pittsburgh, USA
Francois Rheault	Université de Sherbrooke, Canada
Jan Klein	Fraunhofer MEVIS, Germany
Jinglei Lv	University of Sydney, Australia
Kurt G. Schilling	Vanderbilt University, USA
Lianrui Zuo	Vanderbilt University, USA
Marco Pizzolato	Technical University of Denmark, Denmark
Marta M. Correia	University of Cambridge, UK
Matteo Figini	University College London, UK
Nazirah Mohd Khairi	Vanderbilt University, USA
Pew-Thian Yap	University of North Carolina at Chapel Hill, USA
Samuel Deslauriers-Gauthier	Université Côte d'Azur, Inria, France
Silvia De Santis	Instituto de Neurociencias (CSIC-UMH), Spain
Simona Schiavi	ASG Superconductors S.p.A., Italy

Suyash P. Awate	Indian Institute of Technology Bombay, India
Thomas Schultz	B-IT and University of Bonn, Germany
Tomasz Pieciak	Universidad de Valladolid, Spain
Ye Wu	Nanjing University of Science and Technology, China
ZhuangJian Yang	University College London, UK
Zihao Tang	University of Sydney, Australia

Keynote speakers

Susie Y. Huang	MGH and Harvard Medical School, USA
Jelle Veraart	NYU Grossman School of Medicine, USA

Contents

From Fiber Tracts to Tumor Spread: Biophysical Modeling of Butterfly Glioma Growth Using Diffusion Tensor Imaging

Jonas Weidner[1,2]([⊠]), Ivan Ezhov[1], Michal Balcerak[3], André Datchev[1], Lucas Zimmer[1,2], Daniel Rueckert[1,2,4], Björn Menze[3], and Benedikt Wiestler[1,2]

[1] Technical University of Munich, Munich, Germany
`j.weidner@tum.de`
[2] Munich Center for Machine Learning, Munich, Germany
[3] University of Zurich, Zurich, Switzerland
[4] Imperial College London, London, England

Abstract. Butterfly tumors are a distinct class of gliomas that span the corpus callosum, producing a characteristic butterfly-shaped appearance on MRI. The distinctive growth pattern of these tumors highlights how white matter fibers and structural connectivity influence brain tumor cell migration. To investigate this relation, we applied biophysical tumor growth models to a large patient cohort, systematically comparing models that incorporate fiber tract information with those that do not. Our results demonstrate that including fiber orientation data significantly improves model accuracy, particularly for a subset of butterfly tumors. These findings highlight the critical role of white matter architecture in tumor spread and suggest that integrating fiber tract information can enhance the precision of radiotherapy target volume delineation.

Keywords: Butterfly Tumors · Diffusion Tensor Imaging · Tumor Growth Modeling · Brain Tumors · Fiber Tracts · Radiotherapy Planning

1   Introduction

Calling a lethal tumor a 'butterfly' is paradoxical. It places the gentle image of a beautiful, lively creature beside the harsh medical reality of a lethal disease.

In neuro-oncology, the "butterfly" label is descriptive: on MRI, an infiltrating glioblastoma can spread from one cerebral hemisphere to the other through the corpus callosum, producing two roughly symmetrical wings of tumor tissue bridging the brain's midline. The tumor invades both hemispheres and uses the commissural fibers of the corpus callosum as a natural corridor for spread [3]. Population-based analysis consistently reports median overall survival below one year, which is significantly worse than typical glioblastoma [8].

Experimental and clinical evidence shows that glioma cells migrate anisotropically, following the orientation of axonal bundles and other white matter structures [2,7,12,19]. Diffusion tensor imaging (DTI) maps the principal direction of

M. Chamberland et al. (Eds.): CDMRI 2025, LNCS 16205, pp. 1–9, 2026.
https://doi.org/10.1007/978-3-032-12837-9_1

water diffusion, which parallels axonal orientation in healthy tissue, and therefore provides an *in vivo* proxy for the preferential paths of tumor spread. Quantitative analyses of fractional anisotropy and mean diffusivity demonstrate that infiltration fronts align with major tracts such as the corpus callosum, corona radiate, and cingulum [10].

Mathematical descriptions of glioma growth have long incorporated diffusion terms to simulate tumor infiltration. The typical approach to include tumor heterogeneity in brain tissue is to overweigh the diffusion within white matter compared to gray matter [14]. However, these models do not include anisotropic diffusion, but rather simply assume isotropic diffusion.

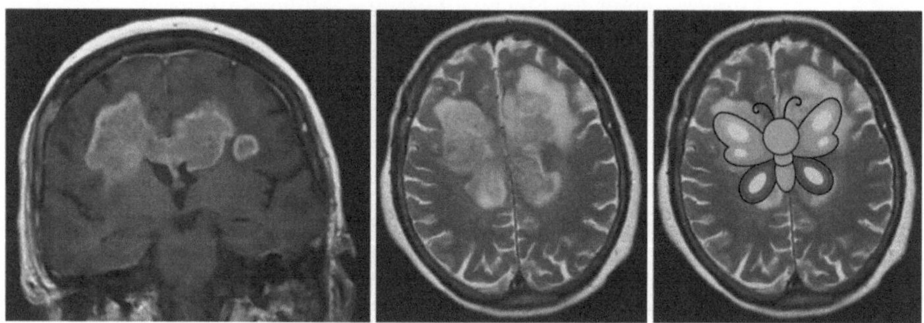

Fig. 1. Butterfly tumors are gliomas spreading between both brain hemispheres. The infiltration follows the brain fiber tracts across the corpus callosum. (Figure adapted from [9])

Successive work embedded the full diffusion tensor into reactionâĂŞdiffusion equations, creating anisotropic models [13]. A slight improvement in patient fit was found by including fiber information. However, only the enhancing part of the tumor was considered, while the surrounding edema was ignored. The growth and diffusion rates were fixed for all patients based on empirical findings and not inferred individually, and only one tumor in one hemisphere was considered, no butterfly tumors. In total, only 10 patients were investigated.

Recently, a hybrid framework that combines shortest path algorithms with classical diffusion to approximate microscopic tumor fronts was presented [4]. By embedding patient-specific diffusion tensors, their model produced elongated, asymmetric invasion patterns that followed white matter orientation more closely than isotropic diffusion alone, and the anisotropic margins derived from these paths reduced normal tissue irradiation while preserving coverage of high-risk regions. However, the prediction is purely path-based and does not consider growth dynamics (Fig. 1).

Here, we investigate the "added value" of integrating fibre information into state-of-the-art tumor growth models to study and exploit the relation between fibre orientation and tumor spread in the brain. Our contributions are the following:

- We propose a novel way to include fiber information into personalized reaction-diffusion tumor growth models.
- We systematically study patient-specific anisotropic reaction-diffusion models in a large patient cohort.
- We demonstrate that adding fiber orientation improves the model fit, strongest for tumors crossing the corpus callosum, the butterfly tumors.

2   Methods

We utilize a biophysical tumor model to describe the growth process of brain tumors. Based on a simple imaging model, we fit the model to individual patients using a state-of-the-art evolutionary algorithm.

2.1   Biophysical Tumor Model

We use the well-established Fisher-Kolmogorov equation to model brain-tumor growth. This model captures the spatiotemporal dynamics of glioma progression through proliferation and diffusion. It enables subject-specific simulation by incorporating anatomical priors and diffusion anisotropy.

$$\frac{\partial c(\mathbf{x}, t)}{\partial t} = \nabla \cdot (D(\mathbf{x}) \nabla c(\mathbf{x}, t)) + \rho\, c(\mathbf{x}, t) \left(1 - c(\mathbf{x}, t)\right), \tag{1}$$

where $c(\mathbf{x}, t)$ is the tumor-cell density depending on time t and location x. $D(\mathbf{x})$ is the tissue-dependent diffusion tensor, and ρ is the proliferation rate.

We can separate the diffusion tensor into an isotropic part and an anisotropic part.

$$D = D_{\text{isotropic}} + D_{\text{anisotropic}} \tag{2}$$

The isotropic diffusion coefficient $D_{\text{isotropic}}$ is characterized by the scalar diffusion coefficient δ and the ratio r of white matter (WM), gray matter (GM) and cerebrospinal fluid (CSF) at each location. Thus, $\forall x : r_{\text{WM}}(x) + r_{\text{GM}}(x) + r_{\text{CSF}}(x) = 1$. The diffusion is assumed to be smaller in GM because tumor cells infiltrate GM more slowly and are assumed not to invade CSF [5].

$$D_{\text{isotropic}}(x) = \delta(r_{\text{WM}}(x) + 0.1 \cdot r_{\text{GM}}(x))I \tag{3}$$

I represents the identity matrix.

For the anisotropic part, we propose a novel way to include fiber information extracted from DTI. We assume a linear relation between measured DTI and tumor diffusion. Therefore, we normalize the raw DTI tensor inside the white matter brain mask to get the standard normally distributed tensor D_{DTI}. This is scaled by the anisotropic coefficient γ. The gray matter diffusion is assumed to be isotropic.

$$D_{\text{anisotropic}}(x) = \gamma D_{\text{DTI}}(x) \tag{4}$$

Note that this formulation allows the fallback into the isotropic case for vanishing γ: $\lim_{\gamma \to 0} D \to D_{\text{isotropic}}$.

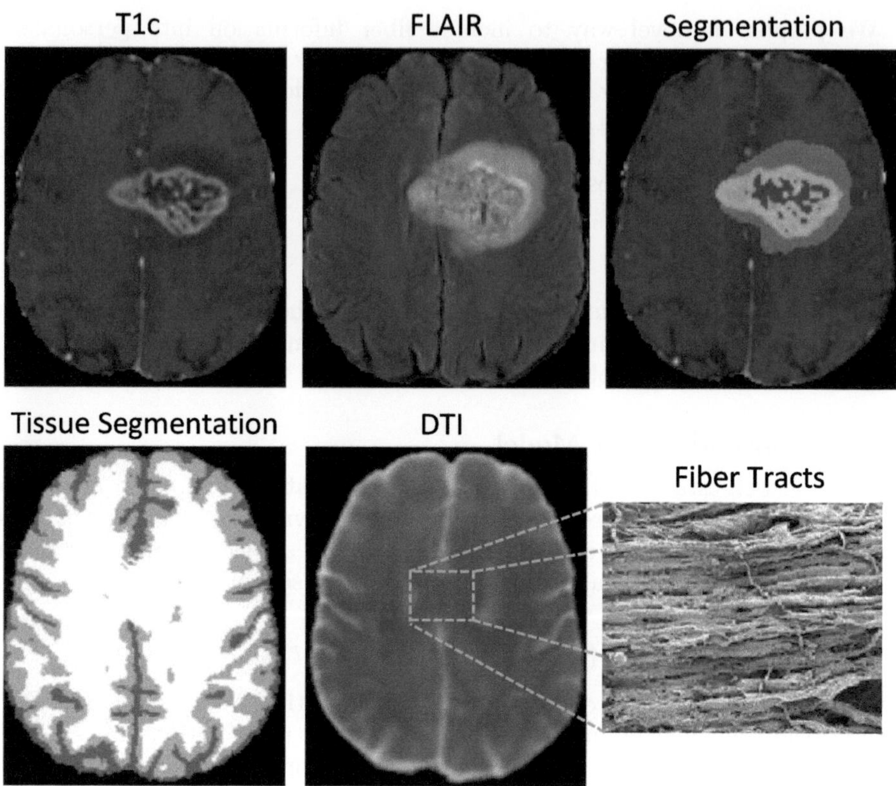

Fig. 2. Preprocessing example of DTI registration. The measured MRIs are shown in the first row. In the second row, we register an atlas brain anatomy onto the patient to get a healthy version of the brain, with the anatomy of the final state. Thus, we can extract pre-tumor tissue segmentation and diffusion tensor imaging (DTI) fiber information. The color coding in the DTI describes the fiber orientation. The corpus callosum (red), connecting both hemispheres of the brain, has the strongest anisotropy due to the dense fibers. (Color figure online)

2.2   Data

We used the publicly available BraTS dataset [11]. We randomly selected 100 single-hemisphere tumors for the baseline cohort. We also curated eight butterfly-tumor cases for focused analysis.

For the biophysical model, we need the original, pre-tumor brain anatomy to reconstruct the growth process (Fig. 2). As these healthy images are typically not available, and the grown tumor in the preoperative image does not allow for a reasonable segmentation of tissue, we register the Human Connectome Project (HCP) atlas [18] T1, which was preregistered to the Montreal Neurological Institute (MNI) atlas [6], into the patient space. This provides a first-order approximation of the healthy brain, but in the anatomical shape of the final state, which allows us to ignore the mass effect and simulate in a steady tissue state. For this, we use the ANTs algorithm [15] to register the T1c image (which typically has the highest resolution) to the atlas. With the same deformation field, we also register the tissue segmentation and the DTI. It is important to mention that for the registration of the DTI, we also need to rotate the tensors according to the deformation field. Therefore, we used the *ReorientTensorImage* function from the ANTs library [16].

This registration provides an estimate of the fiber tracts also for patients without a DTI measurement. We also use this registered image for patients where there would be a DTI available, as the tumor destroys the underlying fibers.

Additionally, we can partly adjust for the mass effect, which describes the tumor-induced tissue shift by using the deformation field from the registration as an estimate.

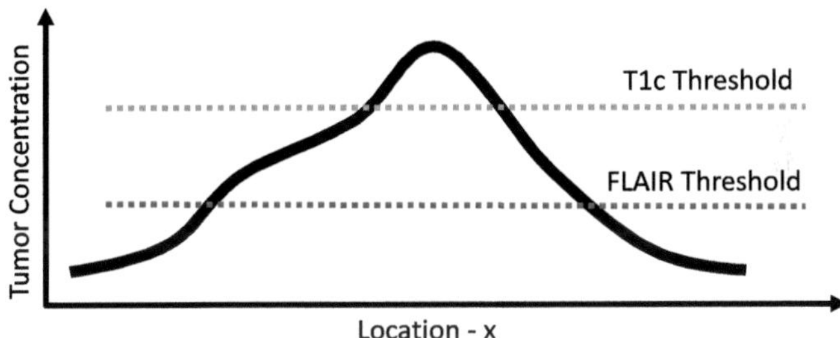

Fig. 3. The imaging functions describe the mapping between continuous tumor concentration and MRI. In this study, we use a commonly used imaging function that is based on the T1c and FLAIR tumor segmentation. We assume that the threshold for the tumor concentration to be visible in the FLAIR image is 0.33 and 0.66, respectively, in the T1c image.

2.3 Evaluation Metrics

We assess segmentation accuracy with the Dice score. Based on our imaging function (Fig. 3), we binarize the continuous tumor concentration to compare it with the measured MRI. We calculate the Dice for the edema and tumor core, which is the necrosis and enhancing part, separately. Additionally, we compare a volume-weighted combined Dice.

2.4 Fitting the Model to Patients

For individualized therapy, the biophysical model is fitted to a specific patient. The forward solver requires the proliferation rate ρ, diffusion coefficient δ, DTI coefficient γ, seed location (x, y, z), and total growth time T, i.e. the parameter set

$$\theta_{\mathrm{orig}} = \{x,\, y,\, z,\, \rho,\, \delta, \gamma, T\}. \tag{5}$$

With only a single clinical scan, θ is not identifiable. Thus, we normalize the final time and optimize $\theta_{\mathrm{DTI}} := \theta_{\mathrm{orig}}\backslash\{T\} = \{x,\, y,\, z,\, \rho,\, \delta, \gamma\}$ instead. For the comparison to the isotropic case, we set $\gamma = 0$ and optimize $\theta_{\mathrm{isotropic}} := \theta_{\mathrm{DTI}}\backslash\{\gamma\} = \{x,\, y,\, z,\, \rho,\, \delta\}$. For the optimization process, we utilize covariance matrix adaptation - evolutionary strategy (CMA-ES) [17] and TUMORGROWTH-TOOLKIT [1] as a forward solver. As a loss function, we use the volume-weighted Dice between edema and T1c segmentation.[1]

3   Results

A qualitative example of tumor concentration estimation is shown in Fig. 4. We find that the anisotropic model outperforms the isotropic model. The anisotropic model approximates butterfly tumors much more accurately, in particular, capturing the transcallosal growth.

These qualitative findings are backed by the quantitative results shown in Table 1. In the large study on single hemispheric tumors, we find that the Dice score is improved by about 1.2% for tumor core and edema in the anisotropic model over the isotropic model. This finding suggests that incorporating fiber information generally improves tumor-growth modeling.

The improvement of the anisotropic model is especially visible for the butterfly tumors. In the butterfly cohort, the Dice score for the tumor core rises by roughly 5%. This underlines the assumption of the strong dependence on fiber information for butterfly tumors.

Table 1. Mean Dice scores with standard error. Comparing the anisotropic and isotropic biophysical models, as well as the pairwise improvement of the anisotropic model on a large cohort of single-hemisphere tumors and butterfly tumors. We find significant improvement ("*" for $p < 0.05$ and "**" for $p < 0.01$ using a paired t-test), for the anisotropic approach.

Tumor Type	Model	Weighted Dice	Edema	Tumor Core
Single Hemisphere	Isotropic	0.613 ± 0.010	0.506 ± 0.014	0.721 ± 0.012
	Anisotropic	$0.626 \pm 0.009^{**}$	$0.519 \pm 0.014^{**}$	$0.733 \pm 0.010^{*}$
	Pairwise Improvement	$0.013 \pm 0.002^{**}$	$0.013 \pm 0.003^{**}$	$0.012 \pm 0.006^{*}$
Butterfly	Isotropic	0.527 ± 0.042	0.384 ± 0.061	0.669 ± 0.028
	Anisotropic	0.550 ± 0.039	0.384 ± 0.067	0.716 ± 0.021
	Pairwise Improvement	0.023 ± 0.011	0.000 ± 0.011	0.047 ± 0.031

---

[1] Code: https://github.com/jonasw247/glioma-inverse-fitting-tool.

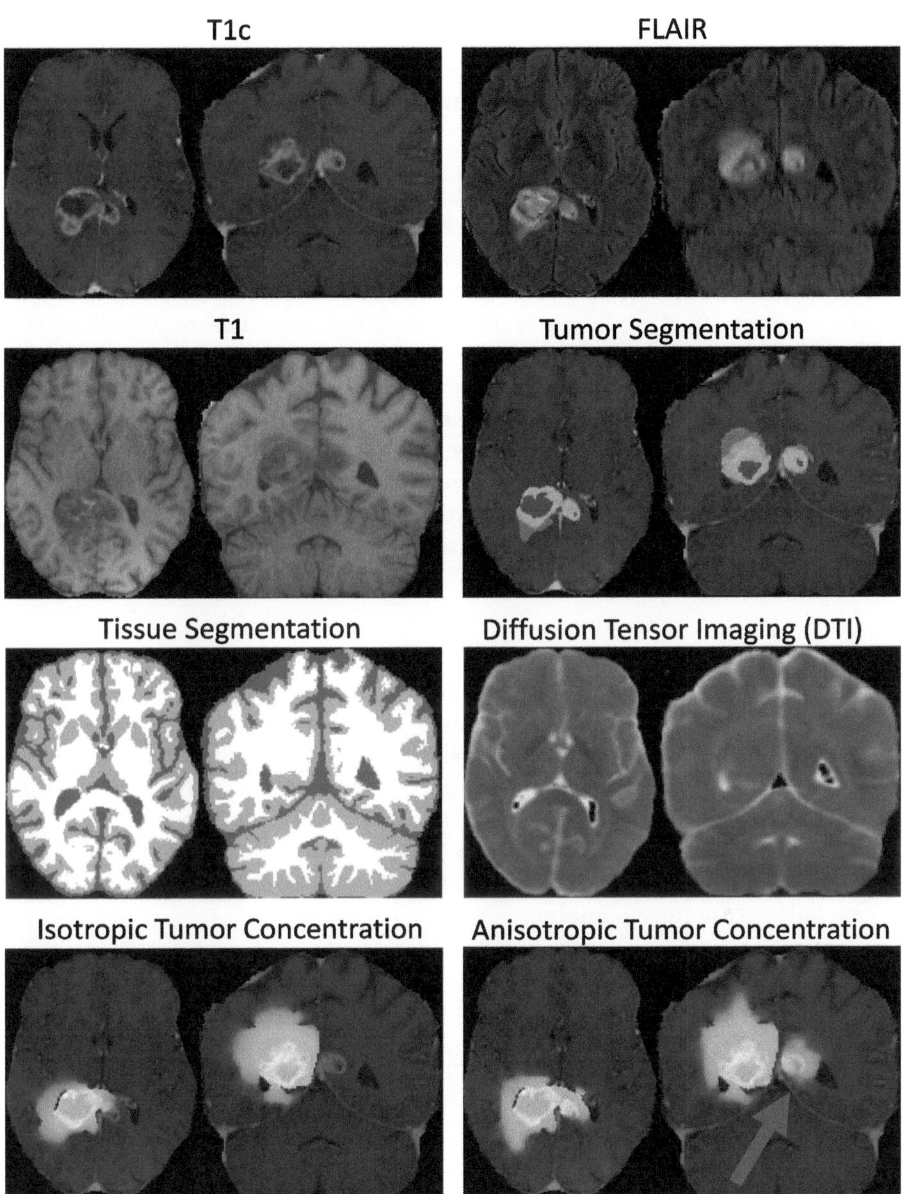

Fig. 4. Example of a butterfly tumor. We show the measured MRI modalities T1c, T1, FLAIR, and the tumor segmentation. In the next row, we display the registered tissue segmentation and DTI, which are used for the simulation. In the last row, we compare the isotropic model with the anisotropic model. We find that only the anisotropic model is able to reproduce the butterfly tumor growth behaviour properly (red arrow). (Color figure online)

4   Discussion

Our results confirm that embedding atlas fiber orientation, warped to individual patients' anatomy, into the Fisher Kolmogorov model yields a significant gain in accuracy, with the effect being most pronounced in butterfly gliomas that traverse the corpus callosum. The modest but consistent improvement in single-hemisphere cases suggests that white matter anisotropy influences tumor growth in general. Thus, our results agree with the observations of [13], extending them to a statistically robust cohort. At the same time, the limited magnitude of the Dice increase indicates that other factors, such as microenvironmental heterogeneity or mass effect, still constrain predictive power. The registration-based recovery of healthy tissue and fibers might lead to minor errors, partially hindering the benefit of anisotropy. Future work should therefore focus on refining anatomy reconstruction and on jointly estimating patient-specific proliferation and diffusion parameters from longitudinal images to further tighten the model fit. For a more precise model of fiber crossings, which are not captured by DTI, microstructure models can provide additional improvements. Based on our findings, learning based or hybrid models, now including fiber information, can be explored.

5   Conclusion

We introduced the first large-scale evaluation of an anisotropic reaction diffusion model for glioma that exploits diffusion tensor-derived fiber orientation. The approach yields statistically significant improvements over its isotropic counterpart, with the largest gains observed in butterfly tumors where commissural tracts dominate spread. These findings support the routine inclusion of fiber information in biophysical modeling and motivate further development toward patient-tailored therapy planning.

References

1. Balcerak, M., et al.: Individualizing glioma radiotherapy planning by optimization of a data and physics informed discrete loss. arXiv preprint arXiv:2312.05063 (2023)
2. Bette, S., et al.: Local fractional anisotropy is reduced in areas with tumor recurrence in glioblastoma. Radiology **283**(2), 499–507 (2017)
3. Bjorland, L.S., Kurz, K.D., Fluge, O., Gilje, B., Mahesparan, R., Farbu, E.: Butterfly glioblastoma: Clinical characteristics, treatment strategies and outcomes in a population-based cohort. Neuro-Oncol. Adv. **4**(1), vdac102 (2022). https://doi.org/10.1093/noajnl/vdac102
4. Bortfeld, T., Buti, G.: Modeling the propagation of tumor fronts with shortest path and diffusion models-implications for the definition of the clinical target volume. Phys. Med. Biol. **67**(15), 155014 (2022)
5. Ezhov, I., et al.: Learn-morph-infer: a new way of solving the inverse problem for brain tumor modeling. Med. Image Anal. **83**, 102672 (2023)

6. Fonov, V., et al.: Unbiased average age-appropriate atlases for pediatric studies. Neuroimage **54**(1), 313–327 (2011)
7. Halperin, E.C., Bentel, G., Heinz, E.R., Burger, P.C.: Radiation therapy treatment planning in supratentorial glioblastoma multiforme: an analysis based on post mortem topographic anatomy with CT correlations. Int. J. Radiation Oncol. Biol. Phys. **17**(6), 1347–1350 (1989)
8. Hazaymeh, M., et al.: Prognostic differences and implications on treatment strategies between butterfly glioblastoma and glioblastoma with unilateral corpus callosum infiltration. Sci. Rep. **12**, 19208 (2022). https://doi.org/10.1038/s41598-022-23794-6
9. Holzgreve, H.: Ein bösartiger Schmetterling im Kopf. MMW - Fortschritte der Medizin **160**(5), 36–36 (2018). https://doi.org/10.1007/s15006-018-0287-5
10. Latini, F., Fahlström, M., Beháňová, A., Sintorn, I.M., Hodik, M., Ryttlefors, M.: The link between gliomas infiltration and white matter architecture investigated with electron microscopy and diffusion tensor imaging. NeuroImage: Clinical **31**, 102735 (2021). https://doi.org/10.1016/j.nicl.2021.102735
11. Menze, B.H., et al.: The multimodal brain tumor image segmentation benchmark (brats). IEEE Trans. Med. Imaging **34**(10), 1993–2024 (2014)
12. Rao, S.S., et al.: Mimicking white matter tract topography using core-shell Electrospun nanofibers to examine migration of malignant brain tumors. Biomaterials **34**(21), 5181–5190 (2013)
13. Swan, A., Hillen, T., Bowman, J.C., Murtha, A.D.: A Patient-Specific Anisotropic Diffusion Model for Brain Tumour Spread. Bull. Math. Biol. **80**(5), 1259–1291 (2017). https://doi.org/10.1007/s11538-017-0271-8
14. Swanson, K.R., Alvord, E.C., Murray, J.D.: A quantitative model for differential motility of gliomas in grey and white matter. Cell Prolif. **33**(5), 317–329 (2000). https://doi.org/10.1046/j.1365-2184.2000.00177.x
15. Tustison, N.J., et al.: N4itk: improved n3 bias correction. IEEE Trans. Med. Imaging **29**(6), 1310–1320 (2010)
16. Tustison, N.J., et al.: The ANTsX ecosystem for quantitative biological and medical imaging. Sci. Rep. **11**(1), 9068 (2021)
17. Weidner, J., et al.: A learnable prior improves inverse tumor growth modeling. IEEE Trans. Med. Imaging **PP** (2024). https://doi.org/10.1109/TMI.2024.3494022, https://doi.org/10.1109/TMI.2024.3494022
18. Yeh, F.C.: Population-based tract-to-region connectome of the human brain and its hierarchical topology. Nat. Commun. **13**, 4933 (2022). https://doi.org/10.1038/s41467-022-32595-4
19. Zetterling, M., et al.: Extension of diffuse low-grade gliomas beyond radiological borders as shown by the coregistration of histopathological and magnetic resonance imaging data. J. Neurosurg. **125**(5), 1155–1166 (2016)

Biophysical Modeling of Intra-Voxel Incoherent Motion (IVIM) MRI Based on Realistic Cerebral Microvascular Anatomy and Dynamics in Mouse and Human Brain

Grant Hartung[1,2](✉), Zhangxuan Hu[3,4], Divya Varadarajan[2,5], Martijn A. Cloos[6], Dominik Schillinger[1], and Jonathan R. Polimeni[3,4]

[1] Institute for Mechanics, Computational Mechanics Group, Technical University of Darmstadt, 64287 Darmstadt, Germany
Grant.hartung@tu-darmstadt.de
[2] Athinoula A. Martinos Center for Biomedical Imaging, Massachusetts General Hospital, Charlestown, MA 02129, USA
[3] Richard M. Lucas Center for Imaging, Stanford University, Stanford, CA 94305, USA
[4] Department of Radiology, Stanford University School of Medicine, Stanford, CA 94305, USA
[5] Department of Radiology, Harvard Medical School, Boston, MA 02115, USA
[6] Donders Institute for Brain, Cognition, and Behaviour, Radboud Universiteit, 6525 Nijmegen, Netherlands

Abstract. Intra-Voxel Incoherent Motion (IVIM) is a form of diffusion MRI that seeks to characterize the motion of microvascular blood under the assumption that this motion of blood is a pseudo-diffusion process that acts like a random walk. IVIM MRI has been applied to estimating tissue perfusion and hemodynamics in the brain and has potential for inferring microvascular architecture. Here we employ biophysical simulations based on the Vascular Anatomical Network (VAN) modeling approach, which provides both realistic microvascular anatomy and dynamics, to simulate IVIM data at a single location in the cerebral cortex. We demonstrate that the microvascular anatomy and physiology yield asymmetries in the pseudo-diffusion of blood and an IVIM signal behavior that is consistent with multiple blood pools moving with different velocities. We also provide estimates of IVIM signal decay with increasing diffusion weighting for both mouse and human cerebral cortex. This modeling framework can help interpret modern IVIM MRI data and help guide new experiments to extract subvoxel anatomical and physiological information from motion-encoded MRI.

Keywords: human fMRI · non-BOLD fMRI · computational fluid dynamics · brain hemodynamics · diffusion MRI · Vascular Anatomical Networks

1 Introduction

Intra-Voxel Incoherent Motion (IVIM) is a classic MRI technique [1] that uses motion encoding to infer sub-voxel microvascular anatomy and physiology. IVIM is essentially a diffusion-weighted technique that uses low b-values (< 100 s/mm^2) to probe water

M. Chamberland et al. (Eds.): CDMRI 2025, LNCS 16205, pp. 10–19, 2026.
https://doi.org/10.1007/978-3-032-12837-9_2

that is moving faster than typical diffusion processes in tissue. The IVIM technique assumes that the motion of blood within the microvascular network is pseudo-random, or "incoherent," such that the motion-encoding gradients will impose a broad distribution of phases across the moving water protons, leading to phase cancellation within the imaging voxel and reduced signal magnitude [1, 2]. The initial target application of IVIM was to measure water movement through the capillary bed of brain tissue (e.g., cerebral cortical gray matter) both to quantify baseline brain perfusion [3] and, ideally, to measure changes in brain perfusion with functional activation [4], i.e., for *functional MRI*. However, cerebral IVIM has low sensitivity due to low parenchymal blood volume and contamination from cerebro-spinal fluid (CSF) [5]. Thus, IVIM was surpassed by other techniques for measuring brain perfusion (e.g., Arterial Spin Labeling or ASL [6]) or brain function (e.g., the Blood-Oxygenation-Level Dependent or BOLD contrast [7, 8]). Recently, IVIM has enjoyed a renaissance [9] for clinical applications in tissues with a higher blood volume content [10] and for tracking capillary blood velocity changes accompanying brain function [11]. It has some capability to quantify CSF flow [12] with potential applications to measuring brain clearance and "glymphatics" [13]. IVIM may offer more spatial specificity than BOLD, which mainly tracks hemodynamics in veins, by measuring *subvoxel capillary microcirculation* [14] analogous to how high-b-value diffusion MRI measures *subvoxel tissue microstructure.*

IVIM theory applied to measuring hemodynamics rests upon simplifying, yet reasonable, assumptions that may not hold in practice, especially for modern high-resolution MRI enabled by newly available hardware. A key assumption—a random microvasculature, resulting in a zero-mean gaussian velocity distribution—does not hold in cerebral cortex, and the implications of this are not clear. While insights can be gained from random-cylinder models [9, 15], the 'symmetry breaking' of real microvasculature is absent. For example, intracortical vasculature is grid-like, and the capillary mesh is regular. Moreover, blood flows from the pial arteries to intracortical diving arterioles and from ascending venules to the draining pial veins, which cannot be represented in random cylinder models. Fortunately, such asymmetries may present opportunities to extract new, meaningful anatomical and physiological information from IVIM data.

Here, we leverage biophysical simulations of realistic microvascular anatomy to investigate how the cerebral microvascular architecture impacts the IVIM MRI signal. This Vascular Anatomical Network (VAN) modeling approach uses vascular reconstructions of the full microvascular network in a single voxel of brain tissue derived from *in vivo* two-photon microscopy. This anatomy is combined with *in vivo* physiological measurements using first-principle biophysics to predict blood flow and oxygenation throughout the vascular network. This framework has been developed over the past two decades [16–21] and was initially applied to modeling the BOLD fMRI response to neuronal activity [17, 22] as reviewed in Fig. 1.

Mouse VAN models previously predicted an unknown feature of BOLD—a dependence of the BOLD response amplitude on the local orientation of the cerebral cortex relative to the magnetic field imparted by vascular asymmetries [17, 20, 23]—which was later observed in human fMRI data [17, 24]. Another application quantified the contribution of each microvascular compartment to the IVIM signal [25]; while this gave insights into differences in blood diffusivity between compartments, many other aspects how vascular architecture impacts the IVIM signal remain to be quantified.

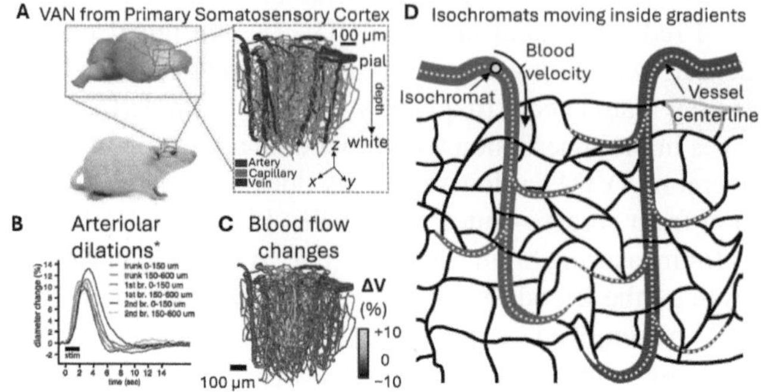

Fig. 1. Review of simulation approach using VAN models. (A) VAN models reconstructed from optical microscopy data from the mouse primary somatosensory cortex (S1). The coordinate directions (x, y, and z) are indicated. (B) Measurements of individual vessel arterial diameter changes accompanying neural stimulation from in-vivo microscopy along the vascular hierarchy. (C) The simulated blood flow response was calculated using computational fluid dynamics. (D) The water particles (isochromats) are then initially distributed evenly throughout the vessels and then travel along the vessel centerline at a rate determined by the blood velocity

Here, we expand the VAN modeling framework to evaluate the assumptions made in conventional IVIM MRI. We specifically test whether asymmetries in vascular anatomy and physiology could be reflected in IVIM data. We compare how the estimated blood pseudo-diffusivity coefficient, D^* (defined below), varies with motion-encoding direction. We also show that the signal decay with increasing diffusion weighting simulated with the VAN model does not follow the standard mono-exponential model used to characterize blood motion in IVIM.

2   Methods

2.1   Vascular Anatomical Network (VAN) Model

We use previously reconstructed VAN models generated from two-photon microscopy of the mouse primary somatosensory cortex [17]. These fully-connected graphs represent vessel segments with edges, each endowed with a diameter and vessel type (artery, capillary, or vein) (**Fig. 1A**). This VAN model has been previously used to simulate hemodynamics during baseline and active states [17].

2.2   Hemodynamic Simulations

To compute blood pressure and flow, we impose strict mass conservation on the system, and set boundary conditions according to previous studies [17]. We enforce the classic

Hagen–Poiseuille equation to relate the pressure drop (Δp) across a vessel to the flow (f) using the fluid viscosity (μ), vessel length (l), and diameter (d):

$$\Delta p = f\, 128 \mu l / \pi d^4 \qquad (1)$$

The viscosity was chosen to match the perfusion flow (flow/tissue volume) to the standard measured value of 100 mL/100 g of tissue/min. The properties representing active states correspond to the peak of the hemodynamic response simulated elsewhere [17].

2.3   MRI Simulations

Table 1: Simulation parameter values.

Property	*Symbol*	*Value*	*Units*
Systemic blood pressure	p_{art}, p_{vein}	105, 25	mmHg
Blood viscosity	μ	1.5×10^{-4}	mmHg $\bullet$ s
b-value	b	1–1000	s/mm^2
Gyromagnetic ratio of water	γ	2.675×10^5	radians/T/ms
Gradient time	δ	8.38	ms
Gradient interval time	Δ	21.5	ms
Particle density	ρ	0.1	particles/μm^3

The proposed MRI simulation environment extends beyond the previous model developed for simulating extravascular signals [17] with a key addition: a particle-tracking algorithm for simulating phase evolution of water moving through the vasculature during motion encoding as summarized in Fig. 1. We simulate each test-particle using classical mechanics as it represents an ensemble of spins that, on average, can be approximated by this "isochromat." This algorithm distributes water particles to each vessel in proportion to the respective volume, using the particle density (ρ) listed in Table 1. A total of 667,242 particles were used for the mouse VAN1 simulations. The particles were then seeded randomly (uniformly) within each edge along its centerline. The particles traveled along the blood flow until reaching an intersection. The probability governing which path to take next was given by the proportional outflow into each down-stream branch. A random number (uniform distribution) determine which downstream segment to enter. The particle locations were sampled at the end of the motion encoding. Motion encoding in IVIM is achieved by applying a magnetic field gradient (in units of mT/m) across the voxel. The magnitude of the gradient, G, is calculated from the input b-value (b), the gyromagnetic ratio of water (γ), and the motion-encoding gradient pulse timing (δ and Δ, , described in the next section) using the relationship

$$G = \sqrt[2]{b / \gamma^2 \delta^2 (\Delta - \delta/3)} \qquad (2)$$

The phase shift accumulation, relative to a zero-phase reference, induced by the motion-encoding gradient is calculated from the differential form of the Bloch equations,

$$\partial \Phi / \partial t = \gamma (rG) \tag{3}$$

where r is the particle's position relative to the voxel center along the gradient direction. We consider only a single voxel, with reference phase at the center of the voxel.

We assumed an idealized image encoding immediately following the motion encoding and neglected effects of T_2^* decay. We then fit a standard single-pool mono-exponential signal-decay model to the normalized signal to estimate the effective pseudo-diffusion coefficient, D^*, of the blood,

$$S(b)/S(0) = e^{-bD^*} \tag{4}$$

2.4   Motion Encoding in the IVIM Pulse Sequence

Our IVIM pulse sequence uses a bipolar pulsed-gradient pair for motion encoding with timing and amplitude indicated in Fig. 2B. Our simplified gradient-echo acquisition uses a single, idealized $90°$ excitation pulse at time $t = 0$ ms, assumed to be played at equilibrium magnetization. Each lobe of the pulsed-gradient pair was applied in a single direction for duration δ, separated by a mixing time. Following the standard convention, Δ denotes the interval between the start of the first and the start of the second gradient lobes. The two gradient lobes have the same magnitude but opposite polarity.

3   Results

We first computed the distributions of blood flow and vessel diameters (see Fig. 2C) from the VAN, and observed roughly 'log-normal' distributions for both (Fig. 2D). The velocity and diameter were weakly correlated (Fig. 2E). The velocity distributions exhibited a nonzero mean and heavy tails along each of the three principal coordinate axes (Fig. 2F). The idealized velocity profile assumed in IVIM modeling is also shown.

One key advantage of our IVIM simulation approach is the ability to track the history of each particle as it moves through the motion-encoding gradient field. Because IVIM models typically assume each proton changes direction several times during the encoding, we counted the number of direction changes during the motion-encoding time (29.88 ms) using several thresholds (see **Fig. 2G**). We found that, even for a moderate threshold of $30°$, the number of direction changes was well above the minimum (5) needed for diffusive-like motion derived previously using a random-cylinder model [9].

After sweeping many b-values (1, 2.5, 5, 7.5, 10, 25, 50, 75, 100, 200, 300, 400, 500, 600, 700, 800, 900, and 1000 s/mm^2), we fit the normalized signal with the standard mono-exponential signal-decay model as shown in **Fig. 3A**. Each principal axis resulted in a distinct signal decay, with the fastest decay in the z-direction (highest D^* value). The lowest b-values appear to have higher diffusivity than the largest b-values. There is also evidence of a sinc-like periodicity; as predicted from random-cylinder models under a non-diffusive, or "ballistic", flow regime without blood changing direction during motion

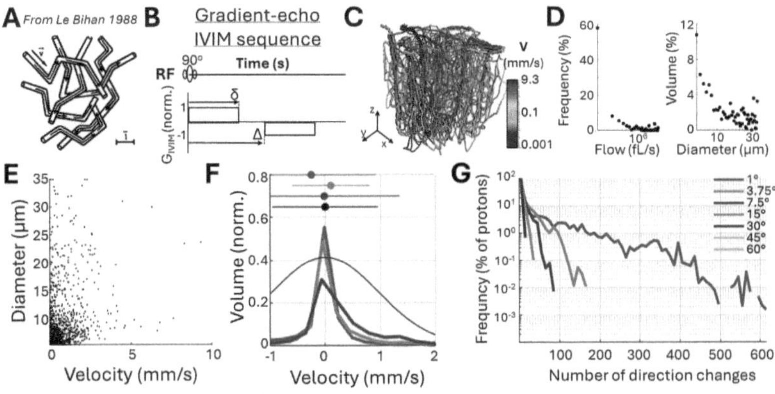

Fig. 2. Revisiting IVIM theory using VAN models. (A) A classic cartoon summarizing the assumed blood movement in a random capillary network. The blood is assumed to change directions many times as indicated by arrows. (B) Summary of the basic motion-encoding pulse sequence, with RF excitation pulse timing and the gradient waveform (G_{IVIM}) defining the timing parameters δ and Δ. (C) The baseline blood velocity based on *in-vivo* measurements is rendered on mouse VAN1. The regular vessel geometry and non-random velocity pattern can be observed. (D) The VAN diameter and flow spectra appear non-gaussian (i.e., log-normal). (E) Weak correlation is seen between the blood velocity and vessel diameter spectra. (F) The distributions of velocity in the x (green), y (blue), and z (purple) directions in the VAN (z is defined as perpendicular to the cortical surface) exhibit a nonzero mean (dots) and heavy tails (horizontal lines represent standard deviation). The commonly assumed zero-mean gaussian distribution (black line) is shown for comparison. (G) The number of times the blood velocity changes direction during the motion encoding (29.88 ms) in the VAN model under different angular thresholds.

encoding [4]. This observed periodicity may reflect blood in the penetrating arteries and ascending veins that run perpendicular to the cortical surface and change direction less frequently.

For comparison, we fit the x-direction motion-encoded signal with both a mono-exponential and a bi-exponential signal-decay model (Fig. 3B). The bi-exponential signal-decay model can capture more pools of water at different velocities. Although this model with more degrees of freedom naturally provides a better fit to the simulated data, it still does not fit the simulated signal decay perfectly.

We next estimated $D*$ from a second, larger reconstructed mouse VAN model, a synthetic clone of the larger mouse model, and from a synthesized human VAN model (Fig. 4). The human VAN simulation yielded a D* value of ~ 16 mm2/s as listed in Table 2, within previously measured values of $7-17 \times 10 - 3$ mm2/s [11]. The differences in $D*$ values from VANs with different microvascular architectures and similar blood velocities raise questions regarding inference of blood velocity distributions from standard IVIM model fits. To test this, we performed simple simulations with analytic solutions using vessels parallel to the motion-encoding direction with equal length and diameter. We simulated a gaussian and a realistic velocity distribution derived from VAN1 (Fig. 5). The mono-exponential model fits data from the gaussian case well at low b-values, but fits to the realistic case poorly at all b-values.

Table 2: D^* values estimated from the VAN simulations.

| | D^* ($\times 10^{-3}$ mm^2/s) | | | | | | |
| | Baseline | | | Active | | | Change |
Encoding direction	x	y	z	x	y	z	(%)
Mouse VAN1	0.7	0.9	2.2	0.8	1.0	2.3	10
Mouse VAN2	2.5	2.4	2.4	3.1	2.9	2.9	24
Synthetic Mouse VAN2	1.7	1.6	1.6	1.9	1.8	1.6	13
Human VAN	14.8	14.5	17.7	27.3	22.1	29.8	68

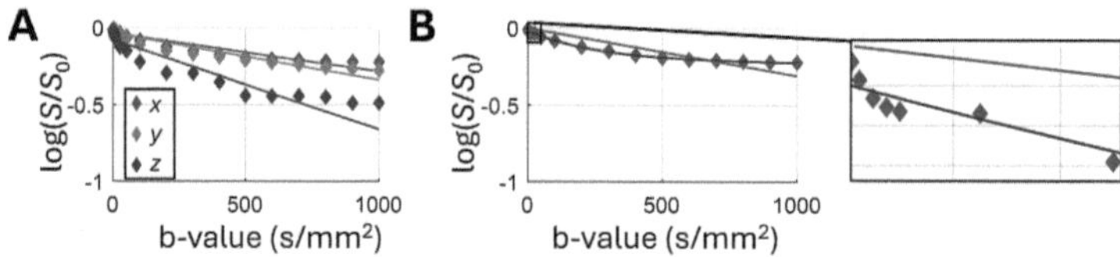

Fig. 3. IVIM simulations using the mouse VAN model yields asymmetry in the estimated diffusion coefficients for x, y, and z directions. (A) The simulated diffusion-weighted MRI signal (diamonds) as a function of b-value (normalized to the signal measured with b = 0 s/mm^2, S_0) for motion-encoding gradients applied in the x (green), y (blue), and z (purple) directions. The signal decays similarly for the x and y motion-encoding directions but faster along the z direction. Fits of standard mono-exponential models are shown for reference (solid lines). The signal along z exhibits some periodicity with b-value, reminiscent of the "sinc-like" behavior. (B) A mono-exponential signal-decay model (green line) gives a poor fit, highlighted by the logarithmic scale along the vertical axis. A bi-exponential signal-decay model (blue line) provides an improved but still imperfect fit, as observed in the inset highlighting data at b-values < 50 s/mm^2.

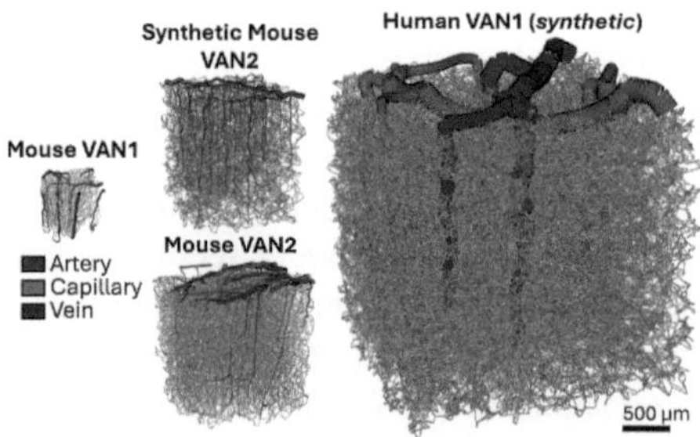

Fig. 4. The three VAN models used for IVIM simulations and for estimating D^*. Two reconstructed mouse VANs (VAN1 from Ref. [17] and VAN2 from Ref. [26]) and one synthetic human VAN (from Ref. [22]) were used.

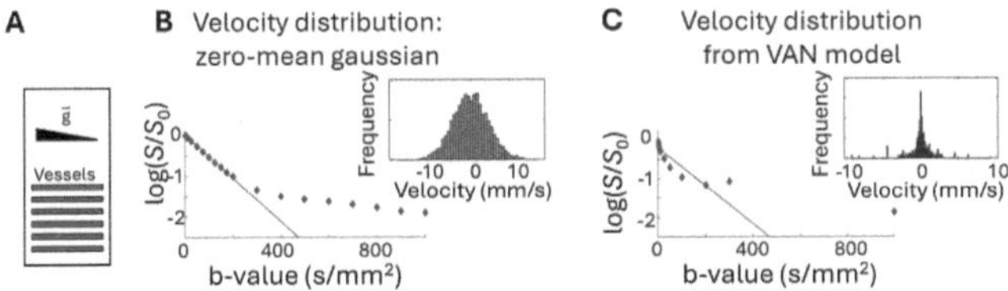

Fig. 5. Examples demonstrating that IVIM "model inversion" to infer blood velocity from simulated IVIM data would be challenging. (A) This process is challenging even with the simplest vascular models consisting only of parallel vessel segments and a single motion-encoding gradient $(\vec{g})$ in the direction of blood flow. (B) Using a zero-mean gaussian-distributed velocity (inset) with a somewhat high variability (standard deviation = 1 mm/s). The IVIM signal decays rapidly with b-value and exhibits a non-mono-exponential behavior, potentially due to phase wrapping. (C) We also enforced a realistic log-normal velocity distribution derived from VAN simulations and fit a D^* value to this as well.

4   Discussion

Here we exploited the anatomical and physiological realism of the VAN modeling framework to test assumptions of IVIM MRI. Specifically, the pseudo-diffusion model of blood assumes the microvasculature is geometrically symmetric with gaussian-distributed velocities. We showed that the cerebral microvasculature has a heavy-tailed velocity distribution with a nonzero mean. To compare with *in vivo* IVIM data, we fit standard mono-exponential signal-decay models to our simulated signals. In mouse VAN1, we observed asymmetries in the fitted pseudo-diffusion coefficient D^*, including higher diffusivity perpendicular to the cortical surface, and a sinc-like behavior in the signal decay consistent with flows with fewer direction changes. We also present, for the first time, D^* estimates from a human VAN model.

Although the human brain is larger and more anatomically complex, the cerebral microvascular architecture in mouse and humans is notably similar in many ways [27]. Still, our estimated D^* values were still quite different, meriting further investigation. We have shown that synthetic mouse VANs estimate smaller D^* values than reconstructed counterparts although investigation of the cause is beyond the scope of the current work. This synthesis-related difference in D^* further suggests the larger estimated D^* in the human VAN are due to differences in vasculature and not the synthesis methodology. We underscore that further *in vivo* measurements in humans are needed to provide more accurate input parameter values and to validate our D^* estimates.

We note that even a bi-exponential signal decay model poorly fitted our simulated signal across b-values, especially at low b-values (<50 s/mm^2). The heavy-tailed distribution of blood velocities may need elaborate signal-decay models with three or more blood pools. Multi-compartment blood pool models pose challenges to IVIM data acquisition due to the necessity of additional pools for tissue and CSF compartments. Future work should characterize the contribution of these compartments and T_2 or T_2^* decay filtering that may affect the relative contributions from arterial and venous blood.

Our simple parallel-vessel model showcased difficulties in inferring vascular architecture from IVIM data. Forward-modeling using VANs enable development of a dictionary of vascular "fingerprints" [28] to coarsely identify vascular architecture from IVIM data. Additional data may be needed from other sources such as (i) different directions and mixing times [14], (ii) multiple physiological states/contrasts [29], or (iii) multiple echo times to separate arteries from veins based on blood oxygenation [30].

Acknowledgments. This work was supported in part by the NIH NIBIB (grants P41-EB030006, R01-EB019437 and R01-EB032746) and NINDS (grant R01-NS128843), by the *BRAIN Initiative* (NIH NINDS grants U19-NS123717 and U19-NS128613), by the German Deutsche Forschungsgemeinschaft (DFG Project number 543670971), and by the MGH/HST Athinoula A. Martinos Center for Biomedical Imaging. Computational resources were generously provided by the Massachusetts Life Sciences Center (https://www.masslifesciences.com/).

Disclosure of Interests.. The authors have no competing interests.

References

1. Le Bihan, D.: Intravoxel incoherent motion imaging using steady-state free precession. Magn. Reson. Med. **7**(3), 346–351 (1988)
2. Fournet, G., Li, J.-R., Cerjanic, A.M., Sutton, B.P., Ciobanu, L., Le Bihan, D.: A two-pool model to describe the IVIM cerebral perfusion. J. Cereb. Blood Flow Metab. **37**(8), 2987–3000 (2017)
3. Bihan, D.L., Turner, R.: The capillary network: a link between IVIM and classical perfusion. Magn. Reson. Med. **27**(1), 171–178 (1992)
4. Le Bihan, D.: What can we see with IVIM MRI? Neuroimage **187**, 56–67 (2019)
5. Kwong, K., McKinstry, R., Chien, D., Crawley, A., Pearlman, J., Rosen, B.: CSF-suppressed quantitative single-shot diffusion imaging. Magn. Reson. Med. **21**(1), 157–163 (1991)
6. Williams, D.S., Detre, J.A., Leigh, J.S., Koretsky, A.P.: Magnetic resonance imaging of perfusion using spin inversion of arterial water. Proc. Natl. Acad. Sci. **89**(1), 212–216 (1992)
7. Ogawa, S., et al.: Intrinsic signal changes accompanying sensory stimulation: functional brain mapping with magnetic resonance imaging. Proc. Natl. Acad. Sci. **89**(13), 5951–5955 (1992)
8. Kwong, K. K., et al.: Dynamic magnetic resonance imaging of human brain activity during primary sensory stimulation.," *Proc. Natl. Acad. Sci.*, vol. 89, no. 12, Art. no. 12, Jun. 1992, https://doi.org/10.1073/pnas.89.12.5675
9. Le Bihan, D., Iima, M., Federau, C., Sigmund, E. E.: Intravoxel Incoherent Motion (IVIM) MRI: Principles and Applications. CRC Press (2018)
10. Li, Y.T., Cercueil, J.-P., Yuan, J., Chen, W., Loffroy, R., Wáng, Y.X.J.: Liver intravoxel incoherent motion (IVIM) magnetic resonance imaging: a comprehensive review of published data on normal values and applications for fibrosis and Tumor evaluation. Quant. Imaging Med. Surg. **7**(1), 59 (2017)
11. Federau, C., Maeder, P., O'Brien, K., Browaeys, P., Meuli, R., Hagmann, P.: Quantitative measurement of brain perfusion with intravoxel incoherent motion MR imaging. Radiology **265**(3), 874–881 (2012)
12. S. Rane Levendovszky, J. Flores, E. R. Peskind, L. Václav\uu, M. J. van Osch, and J. Iliff, "Preliminary investigations into human neurofluid transport using multiple novel non-contrast MRI methods," *J. Cereb. Blood Flow Metab.*, vol. 44, no. 12, pp. 1580–1592, 2024
13. Hablitz, L.M., Nedergaard, M.: The glymphatic system: a novel component of fundamental neurobiology. J. Neurosci. **41**(37), 7698–7711 (2021)
14. Scott, L.A., et al.: Characterisation of microvessel blood velocity and segment length in the brain using multi-diffusion-time diffusion-weighted MRI. J. Cereb. Blood Flow Metab. **41**(8), 1939–1953 (2021)

15. Wetscherek, A., Stieltjes, B., Laun, F.B.: Flow-compensated intravoxel incoherent motion diffusion imaging. Magn. Reson. Med. **74**(2), 410–419 (2015)
16. Fang, Q., Sakadžić, S., Ruvinskaya, L., Devor, A., Dale, A. M., Boas, D. A. : Oxygen advection and diffusion in a three dimensional vascular anatomical network. Opt. Express **16**(22), 22 (2008)
17. Gagnon, L., et al.: Quantifying the microvascular origin of BOLD-fMRI from first principles with two-photon microscopy and an oxygen-sensitive nanoprobe. J. Neurosci., **35**(8), 8 (2015)
18. Lorthois, S., Cassot, F., Lauwers, F.: Simulation study of brain blood flow regulation by intra-cortical arterioles in an anatomically accurate large human vascular network: Part I: methodology and baseline flow. NeuroImage **54**(2), 2 (2011)
19. Hartung, G., et al.: Voxelized simulation of cerebral oxygen perfusion elucidates hypoxia in aged mouse cortex. PLoS Comput. Biol. **17**(1), e1008584 (2021)
20. Báez-Yánez, M.G., Ehses, P., Mirkes, C., Tsai, P.S., Kleinfeld, D., Scheffler, K.: The impact of vessel size, orientation and intravascular contribution on the neurovascular fingerprint of BOLD BSSFP fMRI. Neuroimage **163**, 13–23 (2017)
21. Genois, É., Gagnon, L., Desjardins, M.: Modeling of vascular space occupancy and BOLD functional MRI from first principles using real microvascular angiograms. Magn. Reson. Med. **85**(1), 456–468 (2021)
22. Hartung, G., Pfannmoeller, J. P., Berman, A. J., Polimeni, J. R.: Simulated fMRI responses using human vascular anatomical network models with varying architecture and dynamics. In: Proceeds of the International Society for Magnetic Resonance in Medicine, London, UK (2022)
23. Scheffler, K., Engelmann, J., Heule, R.: BOLD sensitivity and vessel size specificity along CPMG and GRASE echo trains. Magn. Reson. Med. **86**(4), 2076–2083 (2021)
24. Viessmann, O., Tian, Q., Bernier, M., Polimeni, J.R.: Static and dynamic BOLD fMRI components along white matter fibre tracts and their dependence on the orientation of the local diffusion tensor axis relative to the B0-field. J. Cereb. Blood Flow Metab. **42**(10), 1905–1919 (2022)
25. Phi Van, V., Schmid, F., Spinner, G., Kozerke, S., Federau, C.: Simulation of intravoxel incoherent perfusion signal using a realistic capillary network of a mouse brain. NMR Biomed. **34**(7), e4528 (2021)
26. Blinder, P., Tsai, P. S., Kaufhold, J. P., Knutsen, P. M., Suhl, H., Kleinfeld, D. : The cortical angiome: an interconnected vascular network with noncolumnar patterns of blood flow. Nat. Neurosci. **16**(7), 7 (2013)
27. Smith, A.F., et al.: Brain capillary networks across species: a few simple organizational requirements are sufficient to reproduce both structure and function. Front. Physiol. **10**, 233 (2019)
28. Christen, T., et al.: MR vascular fingerprinting: A new approach to compute cerebral blood volume, mean vessel radius, and oxygenation maps in the human brain. Neuroimage **89**, 262–270 (2014)
29. Christen, T., et al.: Quantitative MR estimates of blood oxygenation based on T2*: a numerical study of the impact of model assumptions. Magn. Reson. Med. **67**(5), 1458–1468 (2012)
30. Hu, Z., et al. Characterization of human brain IVIM signal using two-dimensional T2-diffusivity spectrum analysis based on multi-echo diffusion MRI. In: International Society of Magnetic Resonance in Medicine (2025)

Progressive Axonal Degeneration in White Matter Pathways Traversing Peritumoral Penumbra in Frontotemporal Glioma

Patryk Filipiak[1]([✉]) [iD], Timothy M. Shepherd[1] [iD], Dimitris G. Placantonakis[2] [iD], Jelle Veraart[1] [iD], Fernando E. Boada[3] [iD], and Steven H. Baete[1] [iD]

[1] Center for Advanced Imaging Innovation and Research (CAI2R), Department of Radiology, NYU Langone Health, New York, NY, USA
`patryk.filipiak@nyulangone.org`
[2] Department of Neurosurgery, Perlmutter Cancer Center, Neuroscience Institute, Kimmel Center for Stem Cell Biology, NYU Langone Health, New York, NY, USA
[3] Radiological Sciences Laboratory and Molecular Imaging Program at Stanford, Department of Radiology, Stanford University, Stanford, CA, USA

Abstract. Optimal treatment of glioma has been a subject of debate over the last few decades, since maximal resection can improve survival, whereas preservation of functional peritumoral brain tissue minimizes the risk of postoperative neurological deficits. Our preliminary study uses tractography and neural tissue microstructure modeling based on diffusion MRI to quantify progressive axonal degeneration in proximity to frontotemporal glioma. For this, we sample major white matter pathways that traverse peritumoral penumbra at two time points. The results show a pattern of decreased intra-axonal water fraction beyond anatomical MRI abnormalities, which may indicate a tumor invasion of normal-appearing white matter that potentially advocates supratotal resection.

Keywords: White matter fibers tractography · Brain tissue microstructure · Glioma · Diffusion MRI

1   Introduction

Surgical resection of glioma is typically performed with a margin of surrounding tissue to improve survival [30]. For an optimal outcome, neurosurgeons need to maximize the resection volume, while safeguarding nearby eloquent brain structures to lower the risk of postoperative neurological deficits [7,36].

Prior to surgery, anatomical MRI sequences, such as T1-, T2-, or Fluid-Attenuated Inversion Recovery (FLAIR) T2-weighted images, are commonly used to evaluate gliomas and surrounding tissue [33]. However, White Matter (WM) degeneration induced by glioma may extend beyond anatomical MRI abnormalities [9,29], justifying the need for supratotal resection [19], which involves removing more brain tissue than appears pathological on imaging scans.

M. Chamberland et al. (Eds.): CDMRI 2025, LNCS 16205, pp. 20–29, 2026.
https://doi.org/10.1007/978-3-032-12837-9_3

Several studies have reported that glioma cells migrate along WM fibers [15, 28,37]. Although the exact mechanisms of tumor progression remain unclear, researchers observed that brain neoplasms often damage the myelin sheath and invade the impacted axons [9,37,42]. Aiming to quantify this behavior, our preliminary study focused on axonal degeneration in two major WM pathways associated with language, namely Arcuate Fasciculus (AF) and Superior Longitudinal Fasciculus III (SLF3). Both these fascicles traversed the peritumoral zone outside FLAIR hyperintensity in 7 patients with frontotemporal glioma. All patients underwent two surgical resections within less than 7 years, which gave us the opportunity to observe long-term microstructure changes in peritumoral WM, using clinical diffusion MRI (dMRI) acquired prior to each surgery.

As a result, we identified a peritumoral penumbra of normal-appearing WM with a decreased intra-axonal water fraction derived from dMRI signal. A spatial pattern consistent with axonal degeneration with progression between the scans was visible in both studied WM pathways, which may indicate a tumor invasion that potentially advocates supratotal resection

2   Methods

This retrospective study was approved by the Internal Review Board (IRB) of NYU Langone Health (protocol number i18-00124). Access to previously collected anonymized data did not require additional consent from the participants.

2.1   Data Acquisition

We considered preoperative MRI of 7 patients (3 females, 4 males) aged 33 ± 8 y/o (mean$\pm$std at baseline), acquired in our imaging center using 3T Siemens MAGNETOM scanners (Erlangen, Germany). The Diffusion-Weighted Images (DWIs) were sampled at 2 b-shells (details given in Table 1). The echo times (TE) varied

Table 1. Patients enrolled in the study, tumor types and their locations in either left (L) or right (R) hemisphere, diffusion sampling schemes used at the preoperative time points t_0 (primary surgery) and t_1 (repeat surgery), and the time intervals between t_0 and t_1 (in months).

#	Age	Sex	Tumor type	L/R	b-values at t_0	b-values at t_1	$t_1 - t_0$
1	48	M	Astrocytoma	L	20×1000, 60×2000	20×1000, 60×2500	81 months
2	29	M	Astrocytoma	L	20×1000, 60×2500	60×1000, 60×2500	23 months
3	31	F	Astrocytoma	L	20×1000, 60×2000	20×1000, 60×2500	59 months
4	32	M	Astrocytoma	L	20×1000, 60×2000	20×1000, 60×2000	19 months
5	41	M	Astrocytoma	R	20×1000, 60×2000	20×1000, 60×2500	29 months
6	24	F	Astrocytoma	R	20×1000, 60×2000	20×1000, 60×2000	24 months
7	28	F	Astrocytoma	R	20×1000, 60×2500	20×1000, 60×2500	46 months

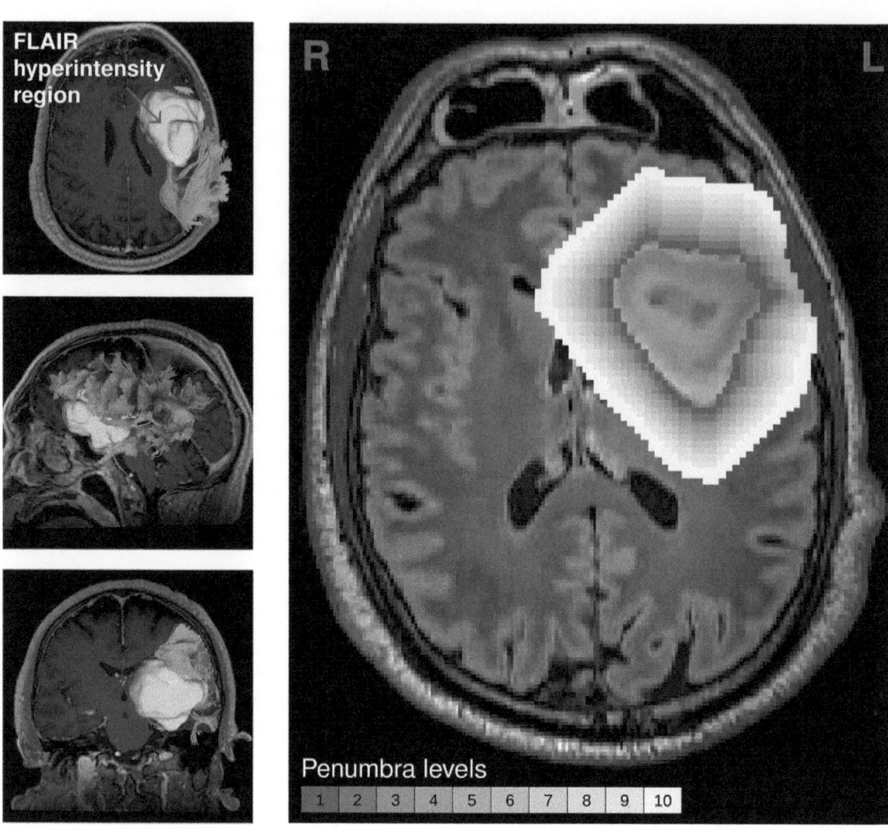

(a) AF & SLF3   (b) 10-level penumbra

Fig. 1. 48-year-old male diagnosed with left diffuse astrocytoma (WHO grade 2) infiltrating the language brain area: (a) Arcuate Fasciculus (AF, orange) and Superior Longitudinal Fasciculus III (SLF3, blue) traversing peritumoral zone, (b) FLAIR hyperintensity surrounded by 10-level penumbra. (Color figure online)

between 92 and 96 ms, although remained constant within each imaging session. The voxel sizes were either $2.0 \times 2.0 \times 2.0$, $1.7 \times 1.7 \times 3.0$, or $2.5 \times 2.5 \times 2.5\,\mathrm{mm}^3$.

All patients were diagnosed with frontotemporal astrocytoma (a common subtype of glioma [33]) WHO grade 2 or 3, for which they underwent two consecutive surgical resections. In each case, we refer to the time of scan immediately preceding the primary surgery as t_0, and preceding the repeat surgery as t_1. The intervals between t_0 and t_1 spanned 23–81 months (mean±std = 40±23 months).

2.2 Data Processing

Preprocessing. We used MRtrix3 [31] with the pipeline including Marchenko-Pastur PCA denoising (`dwidenoise`) [35] followed by removal of Gibbs ringing (`mrdegibbs`) [18], B1 field inhomogeneity (`dwibiascorrect ants`) [32], motion and eddy current artifacts (`dwifslpreproc`) [2]. After these steps, we resliced the images (`mrgrid` interpolation with Gaussian smoothing) to ensure consistent isotropic $2\times2\times2\,\mathrm{mm}^3$ voxel size across all DWIs.

Microstructure modeling. We quantified axonal degeneration by estimating the intra-axonal water fraction from DWIs [5,38]. Given the 2-shell dMRI sampling scheme with $b \leq 2500$ s/mm^2 (Table 1), we were able to fit the following biophysical models of WM:

- **WMTI** – White Matter Tract Integrity [12,20] – implemented in Diffusion parameter EStImation with Gibbs and NoisE Removal (DESIGNER) [1], where the intra-axonal water fraction is referred to as AWF (Axonal Water Fraction).
- **NODDI** – Neurite Orientation Dispersion and Density Imaging [44] – implemented in Diffusion Microstructure Imaging in Python (Dmipy) [11], where the intra-axonal water fraction is referred to as NDI (Neurite Density Index).

WM Fibers Reconstruction. To reconstruct WM fibers, some of which were likely affected by brain tumor, we used Orientation Distribution Function Fingerprinting (ODF-FP) [3]—a dictionary-based technique with demonstrated robustness to biological confounds [13,14]. For this, we generated an ODF-dictionary containing 10^6 elements (i.e., one million) with $0 \leq N_j \leq 3$ fibers per voxel and the microstructure parameters distributed uniformly in their default ranges. We then chose empirically the spurious fibers penalty factor $\lambda = 2 \cdot 10^{-5}$ and the anisotropy boosting factor $\mu = 0.1$ [13].

Tractography. We applied the Euler's-method-based deterministic tractography algorithm [4] implemented in DSI Studio [40]. As the stopping criterion, we set the threshold on Quantitative Anisotropy (QA) [40,41] at 0.10. Additionally, we limited the number of random seeds to 1 million, we set the maximum turning angle of 60°, and restricted the streamline lengths to the range between 30 and 200 mm. To dissect AF and SLF3 (Fig. 1a), we used the atlas-based tracking in DSI Studio [39] with the tolerance of 50 mm to accommodate for the anatomical changes due to tumor. Having these, we created binary maps of voxels traversed by AF or SLF3.

Penumbra. We manually drew 3-dimensional Regions Of Interest (ROIs) containing FLAIR hyperintensities, then registered them linearly in DSI-Studio to the respective DWIs. Next, we generated 10-level penumbras ($10 \times 2 = 20$ mm thick) using repetitive applications of the binary mask dilation filter in MRtrix3 (`maskfilter dilate`) as shown in Fig. 1b.

Evaluation. For each patient, we intersected the intra-axonal water fraction maps (either AWF or NDI) with the binary masks of voxels pertaining to AF and SLF3 in both hemispheres. Next, we computed the respective averages and

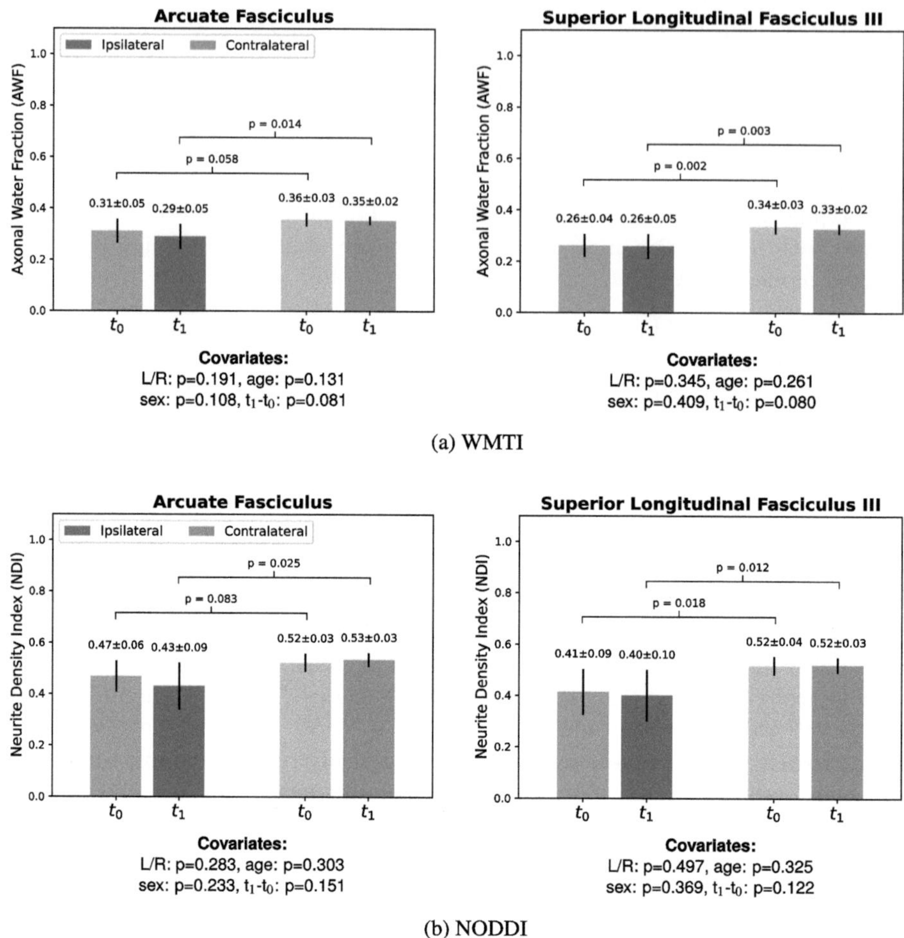

(a) WMTI

(b) NODDI

Fig. 2. Intra-axonal water fractions computed along the ipsi- and contralateral Arcuate Fasciculus (left) and Superior Longitudinal Fasciculus III (right) using (a) White Matter Tract Integrity (WMTI) and (b) Neurite Orientation Dispersion and Density Imaging (NODDI). The bars present averages and standard deviations of 7 patients, measured at two preoperative time points t_0 (primary surgery) and t_1 (repeat surgery).

standard deviations over the masked regions. Note that masking with the WM tracts decreased heterogeneity of the peritumoral tissue and improved stability of our evaluation.

We compared the ipsi- and contralateral distributions of the intra-axonal water fractions using the analysis of covariance (ANCOVA) at the significance level $\alpha = 0.05$. As covariates, we considered: hemisphere where the tumor was located, the patients' age and sex, and the time interval between t_0 and t_1.

Finally, we intersected the intra-axonal water fraction maps with 1-, 2-, ..., 10-level penumbras. For each tract and each metric, we selected the penumbra level with the highest discrepancy between t_0 and t_1, then computed the two-sided t-test statistics at the significance level $\alpha = 0.05$ with the null hypothesis that the respective intra-axonal water fractions were no different.

3   Results

Considerable differences between the ipsi- and contralateral hemispheres were visible at the fascicle level (Fig. 2). On average, the intra-axonal water fractions (both AWF and NDI) of the ipsilateral AF and SLF3 were lower than their contralateral counterparts. Over time, both averaged metrics either decreased (i.e., the values were lower at t_1 than at t_0) or remained roughly unchanged. The ANCOVA test demonstrated statistical significance ($p < 0.05$) in most comparisons between the ipsi- and contralateral hemispheres. The time interval between the scans also had a relatively high impact on the results ($0.08 \leq p \leq 0.15$), whereas age, sex, and location of the tumor (in either left or right hemisphere) were negligible (Fig. 2).

As expected, the drop of the intra-axonal water fraction was most pronounced in proximity to tumor. Both AWF (Fig. 3a) and NDI curves (Fig. 3b) formed a slope stretching between the penumbra levels 1 and 5 (i.e., up to 10 mm away from the the FLAIR hyperintensity), until they converged and remained stable along the following levels. The longitudinal change was present in all studied cases, although only in AF the difference reached statistical significance ($p = 0.037$ for AWF).

Figure 3 also shows that the shapes of the intra-axonal water fraction curves were the same at t_0 (before any surgical interventions) and t_1 (after the primary resection), which suggests biological rather than medical underpinnings of the observed spatial pattern.

4   Discussion

The mechanism of glioma progression remains insufficiently understood [15,25]. Recently, the so-called *tumor–brain interactions* [10,25], including brain plasticity [8,24] and tumor invasion patterns [21,26], have drawn attention of researchers studying glioma cell proliferation. In this context, the optimal resection volume is the subject of ongoing debate [6,23,34], since maximal resection can improve progression-free survival [16], whereas preservation of functional peritumoral brain tissue minimizes the risk of postoperative neurological deficits [22].

4.1   Axonal Degeneration in Proximity to Tumor

Our study aimed to probe noninvasively the spatiotemporal microstructural changes associated with tumor invasion of normal-appearing WM in peritumoral penumbra. The observed decrease of the intra-axonal water fraction in

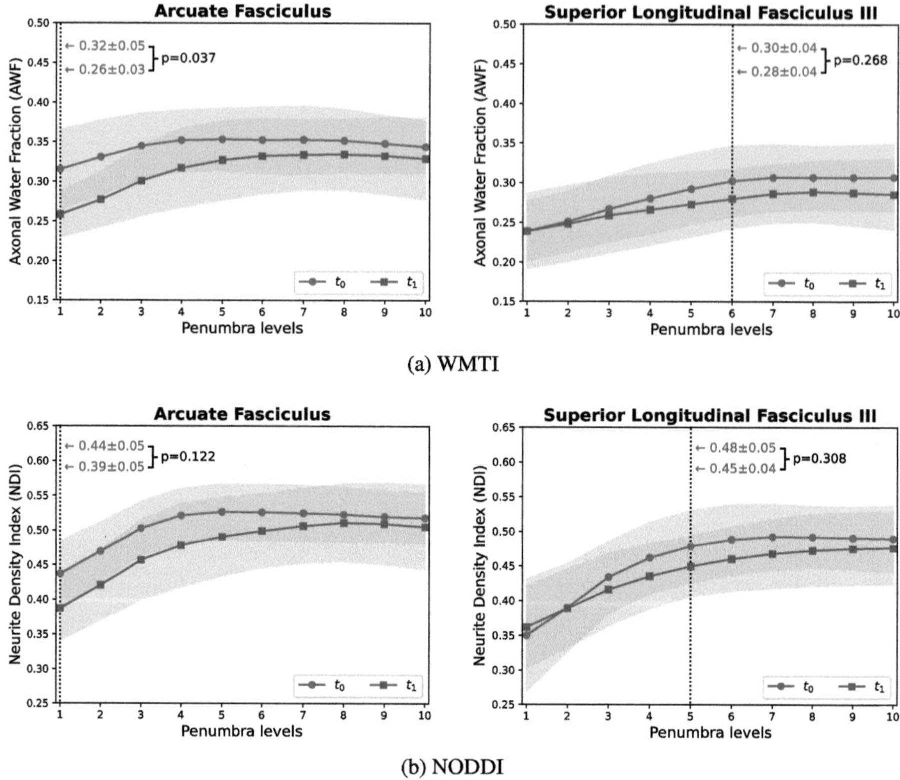

Fig. 3. Fiber fractions along Arcuate Fasciculus (left) and Superior Longitudinal Fasciculus III (right) at various peritumoral penumbra levels, computed using (a) White Matter Tract Integrity (WMTI) and (b) Neurite Orientation Dispersion and Density Imaging (NODDI). The plots present averages and standard deviations of 7 patients, measured at two preoperative time points t_0 (primary surgery) and t_1 (repeat surgery). The dotted lines mark the highest discrepancies between t_0 and t_1 with the averages and standard deviations given at the top.

the ipsilateral AF and SLF3 aligns with the glioma invasion pattern along myelinated WM tracts reported earlier [15,28,37]. The drop of AWF and NDI, which occurred predominantly in the innermost penumbra levels and progressed between the consecutive scans, was consistent with axonal degeneration that can be attributed to tumor infiltration. This result resonates with the concept of supratotal resection to maximize the progression-free survival [27,43], since the observed axonal degeneration appeared outside FLAIR hyperintensity. Upon further validation, spatiotemporal changes of AWF or NDI could inform clinicians about the extent of tumor infiltration and help to adjust personalized treatment. However, future work is necessary to disentangle the impact of other potential causes of the intra-axonal water fraction decrease in peritumoral zones, such as neuroinflammation, radiotherapy, or Wallerian degeneration.

4.2   Limitations

The biophysical models of WM used in this study have been frequently applied to quantify pathological changes in the brain due to their low requirements on the dMRI sampling scheme [17,20]. However, it is worth noticing that WMTI estimates the intra-axonal water fraction from the diffusion kurtosis indices at relatively low b-values, which limits the amount of information that can be extracted [12], whereas NODDI assumes constant intra- and extra-axonal diffusivities regardless of the underlying tissue morphology [44]. As a result, our estimations of the intra-axonal water fractions might have been distorted, although the repetitive patterns observed with both studied models lowered this risk. Finally, let us point out that more subjects are necessary to strengthen the statistical power of our study. All these limitations should be mitigated in future work using densely sampled DWIs.

5   Conclusion

We used dMRI tractography and microstructure modeling to quantify progressive axonal degeneration in proximity to frontotemporal glioma. Our preliminary results showed a spatiotemporal pattern of decreased intra-axonal water fraction outside FLAIR abnormality, which may indicate a tumor invasion of normal-appearing white matter that potentially advocates supratotal resection.

Acknowledgments. This project was supported in part by the National Institutes of Health (NIH, R01 EB028774 and R01 EB029306) under the rubric of the Center for Advanced Imaging Innovation and Research (CAI2R, https://www.cai2r.net), a NIBIB Biomedical Technology Resource Center (NIH P41 EB017183).

References

1. Ades-Aron, B., et al.: Evaluation of the accuracy and precision of the diffusion parameter EStImation with Gibbs and NoisE removal pipeline. Neuroimage **183**, 532–543 (2018)
2. Andersson, J.L., Sotiropoulos, S.N.: An integrated approach to correction for off-resonance effects and subject movement in diffusion MR imaging. Neuroimage **125**, 1063–1078 (2016)
3. Baete, S.H., Cloos, M.A., Lin, Y.C., Placantonakis, D.G., Shepherd, T., Boada, F.E.: Fingerprinting orientation distribution functions in diffusion MRI detects smaller crossing angles. Neuroimage **198**, 231–241 (2019)
4. Basser, P.J., Pajevic, S., Pierpaoli, C., Duda, J., Aldroubi, A.: In vivo fiber tractography using DT-MRI data. Magn. Res. in medicine **44**(4), 625–632 (2000)
5. Burzynska, A.Z., et al.: Correlates of axonal content in healthy adult span: age, sex, myelin, and metabolic health. Cereb. Circul. Cogn. Behav. **6**, 100203 (2024)
6. Chanbour, H., Chotai, S.: Review of intraoperative adjuncts for maximal safe resection of gliomas and its impact on outcomes. Cancers **14**(22), 5705 (2022)

7. Duffau, H.: Lessons from brain mapping in surgery for low-grade glioma: insights into associations between Tumour and brain plasticity. Lanc. Neurol. **4**(8), 476–486 (2005)

8. Duffau, H.: Brain plasticity: from pathophysiological mechanisms to therapeutic applications. J. Clin. Neurosci. **13**(9), 885–897 (2006)

9. Duffau, H.: White matter tracts and diffuse lower-grade gliomas: the pivotal role of myelin plasticity in the tumor pathogenesis, infiltration patterns, functional consequences and therapeutic management. Front. Oncol. **12**, 855587 (2022)

10. Duffau, H.: Neuroplasticity in diffuse low-grade gliomas: backward modelling of brain-tumor interactions prior to diagnosis is needed to better predict recovery after treatment. Curr. Neurol. Neurosci. Rep. **25**(1), 15 (2025)

11. Fick, R.H., Wassermann, D., Deriche, R.: The Dmipy toolbox: diffusion MRI multi-compartment modeling and microstructure recovery made easy. Front. Neuroinform. **13**, 64 (2019)

12. Fieremans, E., Jensen, J.H., Helpern, J.A.: White matter characterization with diffusional kurtosis imaging. Neuroimage **58**(1), 177–188 (2011)

13. Filipiak, P., Clarke, K., Shepherd, T.M., Bruno, M., Placantonakis, D.G., Baete, S.H.: Anisotropy boosting improves ODF-fingerprinting tractography in edematous brain. medRxiv, pp. 2025–06 (2025)

14. Filipiak, P., Shepherd, T., Lin, Y.C., Placantonakis, D.G., Boada, F.E., Baete, S.H.: Performance of orientation distribution function-fingerprinting with a biophysical multicompartment diffusion model. Magn. Reson. Med. **88**(1), 418–435 (2022)

15. Giese, A., Westphal, M.: Glioma invasion in the central nervous system. Neurosurgery **39**(2), 235–252 (1996)

16. Hervey-Jumper, S.L., et al.: Interactive effects of molecular, therapeutic, and patient factors on outcome of diffuse low-grade glioma. J. Clin. Oncol. **41**(11), 2029–2042 (2023)

17. Kamiya, K., Hori, M., Aoki, S.: NODDI in clinical research. J. Neurosci. Methods **346**, 108908 (2020)

18. Kellner, E., Dhital, B., Kiselev, V.G., Reisert, M.: Gibbs-ringing artifact removal based on local subvoxel-shifts. Magn. Res. Med. **76**(5), 1574–1581 (2016)

19. de Leeuw, C.N., Vogelbaum, M.A.: Supratotal resection in glioma: a systematic review. Neuro Oncol. **21**(2), 179–188 (2019)

20. Liao, Y., et al.: Mapping tissue microstructure of brain white matter in vivo in health and disease using diffusion MRI. Imaging Neurosci. **2**, 1–17 (2024)

21. Mandonnet, E., Capelle, L., Duffau, H.: Extension of paralimbic low grade gliomas: toward an anatomical classification based on white matter invasion patterns. J. Neurooncol. **78**(2), 179–185 (2006)

22. Morales, H.: Current and future challenges of functional MRI and diffusion tractography in the surgical setting: from eloquent brain mapping to neural plasticity. In: Seminars in Ultrasound, CT and MRI, vol. 42, pp. 474–489. Elsevier (2021)

23. Ng, S., Duffau, H.: Brain plasticity profiling as a key support to therapeutic decision-making in low-grade glioma oncological strategies. Cancers **15**(14), 3698 (2023)

24. Pasquini, L., et al.: Longitudinal evaluation of brain plasticity in low-grade gliomas: fMRI and graph-theory provide insights on language reorganization. Cancers **15**(3), 836 (2023)

25. Picart, T., Hervey-Jumper, S.: Central nervous system regulation of diffuse glioma growth and invasion: from single unit physiology to circuit remodeling. J. Neurooncol. **169**(1), 1–10 (2024)

26. Rauch, P., et al.: Low-grade gliomas do not grow along white matter tracts: evidence from quantitative imaging. In: Brain Communications, p. fcaf157 (2025)
27. Rossi, M., et al.: Association of supratotal resection with progression-free survival, malignant transformation, and overall survival in lower-grade gliomas. Neuro Oncol. **23**(5), 812–826 (2021)
28. Scherer, H.: Structural development in gliomas. Am. J. Cancer **34**(3), 333–351 (1938)
29. Silva, M., Vivancos, C., Duffau, H.: The concept of «peritumoral zone» in diffuse low-grade gliomas: oncological and functional implications for a connectome-guided therapeutic attitude. Brain Sci. **12**(4), 504 (2022)
30. Smith, J.S., et al.: Role of extent of resection in the long-term outcome of low-grade hemispheric gliomas. J. Clin. Oncol. **26**(8), 1338–1345 (2008)
31. Tournier, J.D., Smith, R., Raffelt, D., Tabbara, R., Dhollander, T., et al.: MRtrix3: a fast, flexible and open software framework for medical image processing and visualisation. Neuroimage **202**, 116137 (2019)
32. Tustison, N.J., Avants, B.B., Cook, P.A., Zheng, Y., et al.: N4ITK: improved N3 bias correction. IEEE Trans. Med. Imaging **29**(6), 1310–1320 (2010)
33. Upadhyay, N., Waldman, A.: Conventional MRI evaluation of gliomas. British J. Radiol. **84**(special_issue_2), S107–S111 (2011)
34. Veeravagu, A., Jiang, B., Ludwig, C., Chang, S.D., Black, K.L., Patil, C.G.: Biopsy versus resection for the management of low-grade gliomas. Coch. Database System. Rev. **4** (2013)
35. Veraart, J., Novikov, D.S., Christiaens, D., Ades-Aron, B., et al.: Denoising of diffusion MRI using random matrix theory. Neuroimage **142**, 394–406 (2016)
36. Voets, N.L., Bartsch, A., Plaha, P.: Brain white matter Fibre tracts: a review of functional neuro-oncological relevance. J. Neurol. Neuros. Psy. **88**(12), 1017–1025 (2017)
37. Wang, J., et al.: Invasion of white matter tracts by glioma stem cells is regulated by a NOTCH1-SOX2 positive-feedback loop. Nat. Neurosci. **22**(1), 91–105 (2019)
38. Xu, J., et al.: Mapping mean axon diameter and axonal volume fraction by MRI using temporal diffusion spectroscopy. Neuroimage **103**, 10–19 (2014)
39. Yeh, F.C.: Population-based tract-to-region connectome of the human brain and its hierarchical topology. Nat. Commun. **13**(1), 4933 (2022)
40. Yeh, F.C., Verstynen, T.D., Wang, Y., Fernández-Miranda, J.C., Tseng, W.Y.I.: Deterministic diffusion fiber tracking improved by quantitative anisotropy. PLoS ONE **8**(11), e80713 (2013)
41. Yeh, F.C., Wedeen, V.J., Tseng, W.Y.I.: Generalized Q-sampling imaging. IEEE Trans. Med. Imaging **29**(9), 1626–1635 (2010)
42. Yen, P.S., Teo, B.T., Chiu, C.H., Chen, S.C., Chiu, T.L., Su, C.F.: White matter tract involvement in brain tumors: a diffusion tensor imaging analysis. Surg. Neurol. **72**(5), 464–469 (2009)
43. Yordanova, Y.N., Moritz-Gasser, S., Duffau, H.: Awake surgery for WHO Grade II gliomas within "noneloquent" areas in the left dominant hemisphere: toward a "supratotal" resection. J. Neurosurg. **115**(2), 232–239 (2011)
44. Zhang, H., Schneider, T., Wheeler-Kingshott, C.A., Alexander, D.C.: NODDI: practical in VIVO neurite orientation dispersion and density imaging of the human brain. Neuroimage **61**(4), 1000–1016 (2012)

Streamline Signature Net (SSN): Efficient White Matter Pathway Recognition for Bundles Parcellation Using Path Signature

Renzhi Zhao[1]([✉]), Xin Zhang[1]([✉]), Zihao Tan[1], Jiakun Xu[1], Zhenyu Yang[1], Ye Wu[2], and Xiangmin Xu[1]([✉])

[1] School of Electronic and Information Engineering, South China University of Technology, Guangzhou, China
`eerzzhao@mail.scut.edu.cn`, {`eexinzhang,xmxu`}`@scut.edu.cn`
[2] School of Computer Science and Engineering, Nanjing University of Science and Technology, Nanjing, China

Abstract. White matter fiber bundle parcellation is crucial for understanding brain connectivity, yet faces challenges due to the enormous number of streamlines and the need for anatomically meaningful classification. Existing methods often struggle to utilize the sequential nature of streamlines efficiently and fail to balance local and global feature extraction, limiting their accuracy in complex white matter architectures. This paper presents the Streamline Signature Net, a novel deep learning framework that addresses these limitations. The key contributions include: (1) leveraging path signature transforms and a dual-branch network to encode the geometric and sequential properties of streamlines, (2) implementing multi-scale window slicing to extract both fine-grained local details and global trajectory patterns, and (3) introducing a dynamic attention mechanism to weight discriminative slices within streamlines. Comprehensive experiments were conducted on two public datasets: ORG-800, an 800-cluster white matter atlas, and 105HCP-72, a semi-automatically annotated dataset with 72 fiber bundle classes. Our proposed SSN achieved state-of-the-art performance(reaching 93.53% accuracy on ORG-800 and 88.96% on 105HCP-72). The results highlight SSN's potential for advancing neuroanatomical research and clinical applications, including the diagnosis of neurodegenerative diseases and studies on brain development. The source code and implementation details of the SSN are publicly available at https://github.com/ RenchZhao/Streamline_Signature_Net

Keywords: Diffusion MRI · Path Signature · Tractogram · Bundles Parcellation

R. Zhao, X. Zhang and X. Xu—Corresponding authors, equal contributions.

1   Introduction

Diffusion magnetic resonance imaging (dMRI) is a pivotal noninvasive technique for in vivo estimation of white matter fiber tract trajectories. It uses local water diffusion properties to reconstruct these pathways as streamlines within a tractogram [1], enabling systematic exploration of brain structural connectivity and providing critical insights into neural network organization. The process of generating streamlines is called tractography. Bundles parcellation groups $10^4 - 10^7$ [2] of streamlines yielded from whole-brain tractography into a limited number of distinct but anatomically meaningful bundles, which simplifies data interpretation, enhances visualization, and enables statistical analysis.

The utility of bundle parcellation spans multiple domains. Anatomical bundles facilitate analyses of neurodevelopment [3,4], cognitive performance [5], sex/age differences [6] and psychiatric or neurodegenerative disorders [7–9]. Group comparisons of bundle morphology and microstructural properties further support robust statistical inference in both research and clinical settings [4]. By standardizing tractography data into anatomically meaningful units, bundle parcellation enhances the interpretability and reproducibility of neuroscientific research.

Automated fiber bundle parcellation techniques include atlases based distance comparison [10,11], region-of-interest (ROI) based segmentation [12,13], clustering-based segmentation [14], microstructure map segmentation [15,16] and streamlines classification [13,17–19]. Our study employs streamline classification due to its distinct advantages. Unlike traditional approaches that rely on point correspondences (clustering-based, atlas-based), spatial priors (region-based), this method treats each streamline independently, preserving the natural continuity of fiber bundles. It overcomes two key limitations: (1) information loss during streamline resampling, especially critical in pathological or developmental studies; (2) artificial fragmentation caused by microstructure segmentation constraints.

Prior studies have primarily treated streamlines as point clouds [13,19] or feature maps [17,18], leveraging correspondence-based deep-learning architectures. For instance, the study by [19] employed a point-cloud network with a two-stage training strategy: supervised contrastive loss for encoder optimization to identify outliers, followed by cross-entropy loss for classification. The approach in [13] integrated the PointNet [20] architecture with atlas-based ROI constraints to generate anatomical auxiliary features, thereby enhancing segmentation accuracy. Additionally, [17] proposed FiberMap, a 2D multi-channel feature descriptor, enabling classification via 2D convolutional neural networks. Concurrently, the framework in [18] utilized spherical space frequency features to construct FiberGeoMap, incorporating whole-brain fiber averaged center points for classification tasks.

Despite advances in streamline classification, several key challenges remain in achieving robust and accurate fiber bundle parcellation. First, the inherent sequential nature of these structures has been underutilized. To address this, we leverage path signature transforms [21], a widely used [22–24] mathematical framework for encoding path geometry, and introduce novel dual branch strategies for streamline sequences. Second, balancing local and global feature extraction is critical for capturing both fine-grained anatomical details and overarching tract morphology. Our approach employs inception window slicing to aggregate multi-scale features dynamically. Third, anatomically discriminative slices within streamlines are not adaptively emphasized. By introducing a dynamic attention generator, we enable the model to focus on anatomically discriminative parts within streamlines.

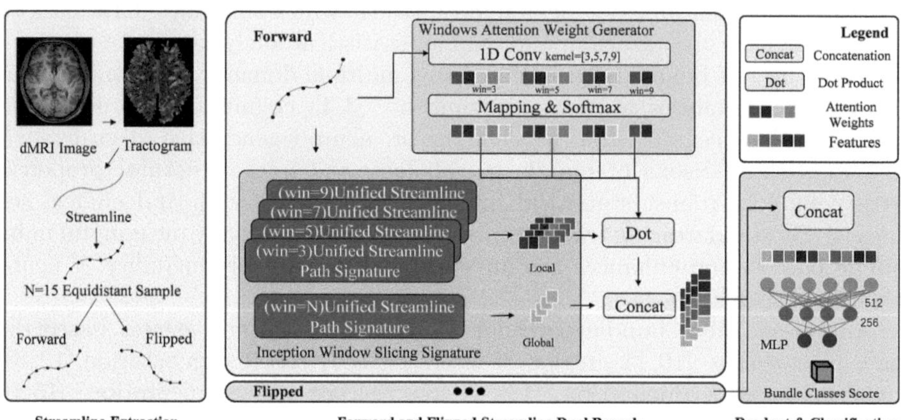

Fig. 1. Our proposed SSN employs a dual-branch architecture. Input streamline data is split into forward and flipped paths first. Each path is fed into an attention-weighted Inception window slicing block (with distinct weights for branches). After feature extraction via operations of inception window slicing signature and attention fusion (as shown in the block), the outputs from both branches are concatenated and processed by an MLP for bundle classification, finally yielding predicted scores for bundle classes.

The main contributions of our work are listed below:

1. Our path-based representation for fiber streamlines enables the efficient encoding of sequential information using a path signature implemented in a forward and flipped streamline dual-branch network architecture.
2. We propose a multi-scale window slicing technique to enhance the aggregation of multi-scale features.
3. By introducing dynamic attention weight generators, we enable the model to focus on anatomically discriminative slices within streamlines.
4. Our unified model SSN(Fig. 1) achieves state-of-the-art performance on the 105HCP-72 and ORG-800 datasets in the field of deep learning.

2   Methods

Our proposed method, SSN, comprises four key components: a forward and flipped streamline dual branch, an inception window slicing signature, a windows-attention weight generator, and classification. Figure 1 illustrates the overall architecture, which processes forward and flipped streamline data through Inception Attention-weighted Signature blocks to extract multi-scale features, followed by a multi-layer perceptron (MLP) for bundle classification. To ensure comparability, the MLP structure aligns with prior work [19].

2.1   Inception Window Slicing Signature

The Definition of Path Signature. Path signature extracts features that encode the geometric information of a path. Let $X : [a, b] \rightarrow \mathbb{R}^d$ be a continuous path of finite length defined on the interval $[a, b]$, mapping into a d-dimensional vector space. For each $t \in [a, b]$, we define the path at time t as $X_t = (X_1(t), X_2(t), \ldots, X_d(t))$, where $X_i(t)$ represents the i-th coordinate of the path X_t, with $i \in \{1, 2, \ldots, d\}$.

The signature of a path can be expressed as a series with graded terms, which includes all iterated integrals of various orders. In practice, this series is often truncated at a finite depth. We define $\mathrm{Sig}_k(X)_{a,b}$ as the truncated version of the signature of X, limited to terms up to depth k, evaluated over the interval $[a, b]$, as follows:

$$\mathrm{Sig}_k(X)_{a,b} = (1, S_1(X)_{a,b}, S_2(X)_{a,b}, \ldots, S_k(X)_{a,b}). \tag{1}$$

Here, $S_k(X)_{a,b}$ denotes the k-th fold iterated integral of the path X, which is expressed as the integral over the interval $[a, b]$, with integration performed iteratively over k variables, as shown in Eq. 2.

$$S_k(X)_{a,b} = \int_{a<t_1<\cdots<t_k<b} dX_{t_1} \otimes dX_{t_2} \cdots \otimes dX_{t_k}. \tag{2}$$

Here, the tensor product $\otimes$ indicates that the integrals are taken over different variables. The result combines the two path increments dX_{t_i} and $dX_{t_{i+1}}$. By convention, the 0th iterated integral is defined as 1, serving as the starting point for the recursive process. The process then continues iteratively for higher-order integrals, where each k-th iterated integral $S_k(X)_{a,b}$ is defined as the integral of $S_{k-1}(X)_{a,b}$ concerning an additional path increment, progressively increasing the complexity at each step.

Unified Streamline Path Signature Layer. In previous work [25], the output of the signature layer was directly passed to the next layer of the network without proper normalization. However, the signature transform results of different streamlines can vary significantly in magnitude and distribution. Since the signature transform encodes the geometric information of a path, streamlines with different lengths and shapes will produce signature outputs with different statistical properties. Layer normalization [26] is suitable in this case because it normalizes each sample independently, which is beneficial when the variance between different streamlines is significant.

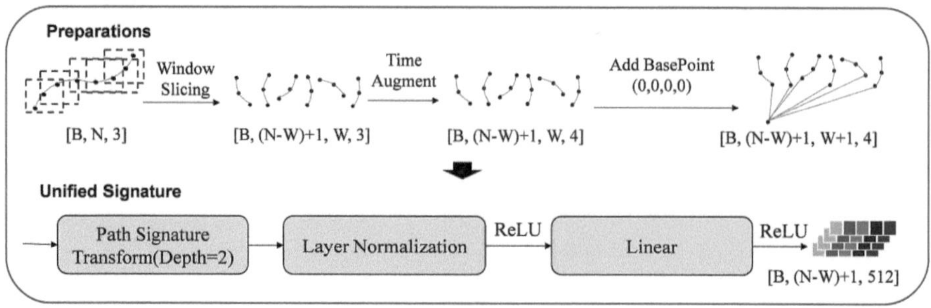

Fig. 2. The illustration of the Unified Streamline Path Signature Layer. Upper part: Depicts data preprocessing procedures, including window slicing, time augmentation, and base-point addition, which prepare the input data for the subsequent signature transformation. Lower part: Shows the unified signature layer that conducts path signature transform, ReLU activation, layer normalization, and linear mapping on the augmented data.

Let B denote the batch size and $N = 15$ the number of points per streamline. As shown in Fig. 2, the 3D streamline data $[B, N, 3]$ undergoes sequential "preparations for signature transform" and "unified signature transform" as follows:

The 3D streamline data $[B, N, 3]$ first undergoes window slicing with stride 1 and window length W, generating a tensor of shape $[B, (N - W) + 1, W, 3]$ to segment the original streamline into overlapping sub-windows for capturing local structural patterns.

Next, time augmentation is applied to the sliced data. For each sub-window, auxiliary time streams are introduced, including the elapsed time since the start $(\hat{t}_i)$ and time differences between consecutive points (Δt_i). In the equal-sampling scenario (uniformly sampled streamlines), $\Delta t_i = \frac{1}{N}$ (constant), augmenting the 3D coordinates to 4D and yielding a tensor $[B, (N - W) + 1, W, 4]$.

Then, base-point augmentation appends the origin $(0, 0, 0, 0)$ as the initial point of each sub-window, converting each sub-window of W points into $W + 1$ points to form a tensor $[B, (N - W) + 1, W + 1, 4]$, which fixes the origin as a reference for the model to learn absolute positional information and address translation invariance.

Finally, the augmented data undergoes a path signature transform (Depth=2) to encode geometric features, followed by layer normalization and ReLU activation [27] to stabilize feature distributions and introduce nonlinearity, and then a 512-dimensional linear mapping with ReLU, outputting a tensor $[B, (N - W) + 1, 512]$ before being fed into the next layer.

The path signature calculations within this block are implemented using the package Signatory [28] and integrated into PyTorch [29].

Inception Signature. In fiber bundle parcellation, both local and global information of streamlines are essential. Local information can capture fine-grained anatomical details, such as the curvature and direction changes within a short segment of a streamline. Global information, on the other hand, provides an overview of the entire streamline's trajectory, which is crucial for distinguishing between different fiber bundles.

Inspired by the Inception block of GoogLeNet [30], we employ unified similarly streamline path signature layers to enable multi-scale feature extraction. As shown in Fig. 1, The raw streamline features are sliced into windows of lengths $l \in \{3, 5, 7, 9\}$, corresponding to different scales of analysis. For a streamline $\mathbf{S} = (s_1, s_2, \cdots, s_n)$, a window of length l starting at index i is $\mathbf{W}_{i,l} = (s_i, s_{i+1}, \cdots, s_{i+l-1})$. Each window $\mathbf{W}_{i,l}$ undergoes a parallel path signature transformation. Additionally, the entire streamline $\mathbf{S}$ undergoes a unified streamline path signature layer with a window length equal to its length, providing global context. The signature features from all windows and the whole streamline are then concatenated to form a comprehensive feature representation.

2.2 Windows Attention Weight Generator

After extracting multi-scale features through the Inception Signature block, different windows may contain information of varying importance for fiber bundle classification. Some windows may capture critical anatomical landmarks, while others may represent noise or less discriminative features. To dynamically aggregate local and global features, we need a mechanism to assign appropriate importance scores to these windows. Since the global information from the whole path signature is already captured and will be processed in the subsequent MLP, our focus lies on assigning attention weights to the sliced windows.

In Fig. 1, we can see that for each window length l, we design a dedicated attention side layer. The architecture starts with a 1D convolution layer that projects the input channel dimension from 3 to an embedding dimension ($emb{=}32$). Subsequently, a scaled dot-product attention mechanism [31] is applied between these embeddings and learnable parameters of the same dimension $[1, 1, emb]$, followed by a softmax activation to generate attention weights that sum to 1. This enables the model to emphasize critical local features, facilitating accurate bundle classification selectively.

These attention weights are then used to emphasize critical local features for accurate bundle classification selectively.

2.3 Forward and Flipped Streamline Dual Branch

Given the importance of leveraging the sequential nature of fiber streamlines, we introduce a novel dual-branch strategy. From the section above, we can learn that the translation invariance of the signature can be removed by base-point augmentation. However, traditional base-point augmentation only emphasizes the streamline's start. We reverse the path and adopt base-point augmentation. In this way, the end of the streamlining becomes the start of the reversed path to be better emphasized. Our approach combines base-point augmentation with path reversal to capture complete spatial information and enhance feature diversity.

Specifically, each streamline is processed in both its original ($\mathbf{S} = (s_1, s_2, \cdots, s_n)$ where $s_i \in \mathbb{R}^3$ represents a point in the streamline) and reversed orientations($\mathbf{S}^r = (s_n, s_{n-1}, \cdots, s_1)$), generating two distinct path representations. These dual-oriented paths are fed into independent attention-weighted inception window slicing signature blocks (no weight sharing between branches, as shown in the Forward and Flipped Streamline Dual Branch) of Fig. 1 to extract forward and flipped path features, improving their generalization ability.

2.4 MLP Classification Backbone

The final MLP classification block serves as the decision-making component of our model. To ensure fairness in comparison, we replicate the MLP architecture from [19], which consists of three fully connected layers with 512, 256, and the number of classes for output units, respectively. Each layer's output passes through batch normalization [32] and ReLU activation [27]. This consistent backbone is used across all models in our experiments, except for DeepWMA [17], enabling a direct evaluation of our proposed feature extraction and augmentation strategies.

2.5 Bundles Parcellation

The inference pipeline integrates whole-brain tractography with our classification framework to enable automated parcellation of fiber bundles. As outlined in the introduction section, we first generate streamlines via whole-brain tractography, which serves as the input to our network.

Each streamline is processed through our model to obtain class-specific prediction scores. A streamline is assigned to a fiber bundle class if its highest predicted score exceeds a confidence threshold of 0.9. This thresholding strategy strikes a balance between classification accuracy and completeness, ensuring that only confidently identified streamlines are included in the final parcellation.

3   Experiment

3.1   Dataset and Feature Extraction

We validated our method using two publicly available datasets. The 105HCP-72 dataset [15] contains 105 subjects with 72 manually corrected fiber bundle classes. Following [17,19], we sampled 15 equidistant points per streamline and adopted the 5-fold subject split from [15].

The ORG-800 dataset [2] is a white matter atlas containing 800 fiber clusters, derived from 1 million streamlines randomly sampled from 100 HCP subjects [33]. This atlas comprehensively covers both deep white matter and superficial white matter regions. For our experiments, we utilized all 793,990 streamlines provided by the dataset[1].

3.2   Experiment Settings

Dataset Splitting. We employed stratified 5-fold [34,35] cross-validation for both datasets:

- ORG-800: 793,990 streamlines split into 635,192 training and 158,798 validation streamlines per fold.
- 105HCP-72: Sampled 1,000 streamlines per class per subject (total 7.36×10^6), split into 5.88×10^6 training and 1.47×10^6 validation streamlines per fold following [36].

Training Configuration. To ensure fairness and efficiency:

- ORG-800: Followed [19] with Adam optimizer [37], learning rate 1×10^{-3}, batch size 1024, and 80 epochs.
- 105HCP-72: Used LARS optimizer [38] with batch size 8192, learning rate 1×10^{-3}, and 20 epochs to handle the larger dataset.

Both datasets used the Cosine Annealing Warm Restarts scheduler ($T_0 = 10, T_{mult} = 2$) [29] and Cross-Entropy Loss. All networks are trained on a single Nvidia RTX 4090.

Whole-Brain Tractography for dMRI Test Dataset. First, five tissues, including white matter, are segmented from the T1 image. Next, the Multi-Shell Multi-Tissue-Constrained Spherical Deconvolution algorithm is employed for reconstructing Fiber Orientation Distribution (FOD). Finally, fiber streamlines are tracked within the white matter using the FOD results. The above tractography procedures adhere to the protocol described in [15], implemented using the MRtrix3 software package [39] with parameters detailed in the Zenodo repository[2].

3.3   Results

As shown in Table 1, the experimental results demonstrate the superiority of our proposed SSN across multiple evaluation metrics and datasets. All models were evaluated using 5-fold cross-validation, with performance measured by accuracy and F1-score.

---

[1] https://github.com/SlicerDMRI/ORG-Atlases.
[2] https://zenodo.org/records/1285152.

Table 1. 5-fold cross-validation classification performance of models. Results are based on optimal accuracy weights. Reported values are the mean ± standard deviation across all bundle categories.

Model	ORG-800		105HCP-72	
	Accuracy (%) ↑	F1-score (%) ↑	Accuracy (%) ↑	F1-score (%) ↑
DeepWMA [17]	72.124 ± 3.021	70.988 ± 3.000	88.189 ± 0.503	87.912 ± 0.637
PointNet [19,20]	91.115 ± 0.088	90.889 ± 0.098	88.522 ± 0.421	88.634 ± 0.453
LSTM [40,41]	93.489 ± 0.035	93.245 ± 0.040	88.700 ± 0.384	88.523 ± 0.529
Transformer [31]	92.131 ± 0.437	91.801 ± 0.446	88.765 ± 0.438	88.812 ± 0.503
SSN (ours)	**93.532 ± 0.063**	**93.312 ± 0.073**	**88.960 ± 0.389**	**88.885 ± 0.486**

For comparative analysis, we use the PointNet model [20] as implemented in [19]. Regarding DeepWMA [17], we perform the same 2D fibermap augmentation as described in its original paper and feed the augmented features into an identical 2D convolutional network following the paper's specifications. We utilized Long-Short Term Memory (LSTM) [40] (with the Pytorch implementation [41]) and Transformer [31] in our experiments. For fair comparison, all baseline models are configured with comparable capacities: both the LSTM and Transformer models use a single encoder layer with 512 hidden dimensions, matching the architecture of our SSN. The Transformer employs classical sine-cosine positional embeddings with 16 attention heads, and its temporal feature encoder outputs are averaged. All models in Table 1 share the same MLP classification backbone described in Sect. 2.4.

The table below shows the results of the ablation study.

Table 2. 5-fold cross-validation ablation study of our Streamline SigNet. This result is based on the optimal weight of accuracy. Reported values are the mean ± standard deviation across all bundle categories.

Model Variant	ORG-800		105HCP-72	
	Accuracy (%) ↑	F1-score (%) ↑	Accuracy (%) ↑	F1-score (%) ↑
SSN w/o flipped branch	93.225 ± 0.162	93.007 ± 0.155	88.909 ± 0.390	88.915 ± 0.448
SSN w/o inception (win=3)	93.234 ± 0.083	93.007 ± 0.082	88.953 ± 0.397	88.899 ± 0.455
SSN w/o inception (win=5)	93.285 ± 0.075	93.054 ± 0.074	88.886 ± 0.434	88.867 ± 0.463
SSN w/o inception (win=7)	93.323 ± 0.120	93.099 ± 0.130	88.849 ± 0.485	88.838 ± 0.510
SSN w/o inception (win=9)	93.432 ± 0.050	93.202 ± 0.056	88.783 ± 0.427	88.814 ± 0.477
SSN w/o attention weight	91.593 ± 0.067	91.338 ± 0.081	88.741 ± 0.308	88.704 ± 0.312
SSN (ours)	**93.532 ± 0.063**	**93.312 ± 0.073**	**88.960 ± 0.389**	**88.974 ± 0.496**

Ablation studies, as presented in Table 2, confirm the efficacy of each architectural element in our model. Flipped streamline dual branch significantly enhances performance by effectively capturing bidirectional path information, which is especially beneficial for identifying asymmetric fiber bundles. The inception window slicing mechanism demonstrates that multi-scale feature extraction outperforms single-scale methods. Window length 3 provides the most critical local features, while longer windows capture global trajectory patterns. The attention weight generator plays a crucial role in dynamically assigning importance to different window features. Notably, removing this component leads to the most substantial decline in performance, underscoring the necessity of adaptively emphasizing anatomically discriminative regions.

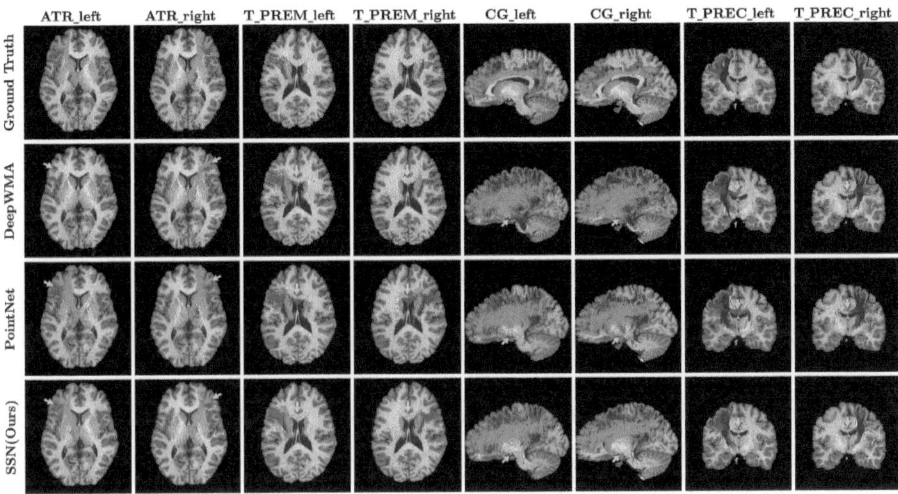

Fig. 3. Qualitative comparison of parcellated fiber bundles for a randomly selected HCP subject (#761957) from fold 4. Inference models are trained on 1, 2, 3, and 5 folds of the 105HCP-72 dataset [15]. From top to bottom: ground truth bundles, DeepWMA [17], PointNet [19], and our proposed SSN.

Qualitative results (Fig. 3) demonstrate SSN's superiority in capturing fine-grained anatomical details and resolving complex fiber trajectories. Compared to baselines, SSN produces fewer false positives and aligns better with anatomical references, particularly in central brain regions. These results underscore the effectiveness of our proposed SSN in modeling white matter architecture.

In summary, our approach achieves state-of-the-art performance by: (1) leveraging path signatures to encode geometric properties of streamlines, (2) using multi-scale window slicing to capture both local and global features, and (3) applying dynamic attention weights to emphasize discriminative regions. These contributions collectively enable more accurate and robust fiber bundle parcellation.

4   Discussion and Conclusion

In this study, we present the SSN, a deep learning model for brain fiber bundle classification, achieving state-of-the-art performance on ORG-800 and 105HCP-72 datasets.

Key innovations include: (1) path signatures and a dual-branch network to encode streamline geometry and sequential properties; (2) a multi-scale window slicing mechanism for combined local-global feature extraction; (3) dynamic attention weights to emphasize discriminative slices of streamlines.

The success of SSN has significant implications for neuroscience research and clinical applications. Accurate fiber bundle parcellation can facilitate a deeper understanding of brain development, cognitive function, and neurological disorders.

Future work will focus on model generalization, integration diverse datasets/modalities, and improving interpretability. This study represents the first path signatures application in streamline classification, with significant performance gains over existing methods.

Acknowledgments. This study was funded by Guangdong Basic and Applied Basic Research Foundation (2025A1515012836), General Program of the National Natural Science Foundation of China (NSFC-62471185), Guangdong Basic and Applied Basic Research Foundation (2024A1515010180), Key-Area Research and Development Program of Guangdong Province (2023B0303040001), the Guangdong Provincial Key Laboratory of Human Digital Twin (2022B1212010004) and National Natural Science Foundation of China (No. 62201265).

Disclosure of Interests. The authors have no competing interests to declare that are relevant to the content of this article.

References

1. Basser, P.J., Pajevic, S., Pierpaoli, C., Duda, J., Aldroubi, A.: In vivo fiber tractography using DT-MRI data. Magn. Reson. Med. **44**(4), 625–632 (2000)
2. Zhang, F., et al.: An anatomically curated fiber clustering white matter atlas for consistent white matter tract parcellation across the lifespan. Neuroimage **179**, 429–447 (2018)
3. Wilson, S., et al.: Development of human white matter pathways in utero over the second and third trimester. Proc. Natl. Acad. Sci. **118**(20), e2023598118 (2021)
4. Karmacharya, S., et al.: Advanced diffusion imaging for assessing normal white matter development in neonates and characterizing aberrant development in congenital heart disease. Neuroimage Clin. **19**, 360-373 (2018)
5. Lo, Y., et al.: Cross-domain fiber cluster shape analysis for language performance cognitive score prediction. In: Chamberland, M., Hendriks, T., Karaman, M., Mito, R., Newlin, N., Shailja, S., Thompson, E. (eds.) Computational Diffusion MRI, pp. 84–94. Springer Nature Switzerland, Cham (2025)
6. Chen, Y., et al.: TractGraphFormer: anatomically informed hybrid graph CNN-transformer network for interpretable sex and age prediction from diffusion MRI tractography. Med. Image Anal. **101**, 103476 (2025)

7. Cooper, M., Thapar, A., Jones, D.K.: ADHD severity is associated with white matter microstructure in the subgenual cingulum. Neuroimage Clin. **7**, 653–660 (2015)
8. Li, J., et al.: A comparative diffusion tensor imaging study of corpus callosum subregion integrity in bipolar disorder and schizophrenia. Psychiatry Res. Neuroimaging **221**(1), 58–62 (2014)
9. Torgerson, C.M., et al.: DTI tractography and white matter fiber tract characteristics in euthymic bipolar I patients and healthy control subjects. Brain Imaging Behav. **7**(2), 129–139 (2013)
10. Garyfallidis, E., et al.: Recognition of white matter bundles using local and global streamline-based registration and clustering. Neuroimage **170**, 283–295 (2018)
11. Dumais, F., et al.: FIESTA: autoencoders for accurate fiber segmentation in tractography. Neuroimage **279**, 120288 (2023)
12. Bertó, G., et al.: Classifyber, a robust streamline-based linear classifier for white matter bundle segmentation. Neuroimage **224**, 117402 (2021)
13. Zhang, D., et al.: Anat-SFSeg: anatomically-guided superficial fiber segmentation with point-cloud deep learning. Med. Image Anal. **95**, 103165 (2024)
14. Mendoza, C., et al.: Enhanced automatic segmentation for superficial white matter fiber bundles for probabilistic tractography Datasets. In: 2021 43rd Annual International Conference of the IEEE Engineering in Medicine & Biology Society (EMBC), pp. 3654–3658 (2021)
15. Wasserthal, J., Neher, P., Maier-Hein, K.H.: TractSeg - fast and accurate white matter tract segmentation. Neuroimage **183**, 239–253 (2018)
16. Xie, L., et al.: CNTSeg: a multimodal deep-learning-based network for cranial nerves tract segmentation. Med. Image Anal. **86**, 102766 (2023)
17. Zhang, F., Cetin Karayumak, S., Hoffmann, N., Rathi, Y., Golby, A.J., O'Donnell, L.J.: Deep white matter analysis (DeepWMA): fast and consistent tractography segmentation. Med. Image Anal. **65**, 101761 (2020)
18. Wang, Z., Lv, Y., He, M., Ge, E., Qiang, N., Ge, B.: Accurate corresponding fiber tract segmentation via FiberGeoMap learner. In: Wang, L., Dou, Q., Fletcher, P.T., Speidel, S., Li, S. (eds.) Medical Image Computing and Computer Assisted Intervention – MICCAI 2022, pp. 143–152. Springer Nature Switzerland, Cham (2022)
19. Xue, T., et al.: Superficial white matter analysis: an efficient point-cloud-based deep learning framework with supervised contrastive learning for consistent tractography parcellation across populations and dMRI acquisitions. Med. Image Anal. **85**, 102759 (2023)
20. Qi, C.R., Su, H., Mo, K., Guibas, L.J.: PointNet: deep learning on point sets for 3D classification and segmentation. In: 2017 IEEE Conference on Computer Vision and Pattern Recognition (CVPR), pp. 77-85 (2017)
21. Chen, K.S.: Integration of paths-a faithful representation of paths by non-commutative formal power series. Trans. Am. Math. Soc. **89**(2), 395–407 (1958)
22. Li, C., Zhang, X., Jin, L.: LPSNet: a novel log path signature feature based hand gesture recognition framework. In: 2017 IEEE International Conference on Computer Vision Workshops (ICCVW), pp. 631-639 (2017)
23. Cheng, J., et al.: Skeleton-based gesture recognition with learnable paths and signature features. IEEE Trans. Multimedia **26**, 3951–3961 (2024)

24. Zhang, X., et al.: Infant cognitive scores prediction with multi-stream attention-based temporal path signature features. In: Martel, A.L., Abolmaesumi, P., Stoyanov, D., Mateus, D., Zuluaga, M.A., Zhou, S.K., Racoceanu, D., Joskowicz, L. (eds.) MICCAI 2020. LNCS, vol. 12267, pp. 134–144. Springer, Cham (2020). https://doi.org/10.1007/978-3-030-59728-3_14
25. Kidger, P., Bonnier, P., Perez Arribas, I., Salvi, C., Lyons, T.: Deep signature transforms. In: Advances in Neural Information Processing Systems. vol. 32, Curran Associates, Inc. (2019)
26. Ba, J.L., Kiros, J.R., Hinton, G.E.: Layer Normalization. arXiv preprint arXiv:1607.06450 (2016)
27. Glorot, X., Bordes, A., Bengio, Y.: Deep sparse rectifier neural networks. In: Proceedings of the Fourteenth International Conference on Artificial Intelligence and Statistics, pp. 315–323. JMLR Workshop and Conference Proceedings (2011)
28. Kidger, P., Lyons, T.: Signatory: differentiable computations of the signature and logsignature transforms, on both CPU and GPU. In: International Conference on Learning Representations (2021). https://github.com/patrick-kidger/signatory
29. Paszke, A., et al.: PyTorch: an imperative style, high-performance deep learning library. In: Advances in Neural Information Processing Systems. vol. 32, Curran Asso- ciates, Inc. (2019)
30. Szegedy, C., et al.: Going deeper with convolutions. In: CVPR, pp. 1-9 (2015). https://openaccess.thecvf.com/content_cvpr_2015/html/Szegedy_Going_Deeper_With_2015_CVPR_paper.html
31. Vaswani, A., et al.: Attention is all you need. In: Guyon, I., Luxburg, U.V., Bengio, S., Wallach, H., Fergus, R., Vishwanathan, S., Garnett, R. (eds.) Advances in Neural Information Processing Systems. vol. 30, Curran Associates, Inc. (2017)
32. Ioffe, S., Szegedy, C.: Batch normalization: accelerating deep network training by reducing internal covariate shift. In: Proceedings of the 32nd International Conference on Machine Learning, pp. 448-456. PMLR (2015)
33. Van Essen, D.C., Smith, S.M., Barch, D.M., Behrens, T.E.J., Yacoub, E., Ugurbil, K.: The WU-Minn human connectome project: an overview. Neuroimage **80**, 62–79 (2013)
34. Pedregosa, F., et al.: Scikit-learn: machine learning in python. J. Mach. Learn. Res. **12**, 2825–2830 (2011)
35. Buitinck, L., et al.: API design for machine learning software: experiences from the scikit-learn project. In: ECML PKDD Workshop: Languages for Data Mining and Machine Learning, pp. 108–122 (2013)
36. Wu, Y., Hong, Y., Ahmad, S., Lin, W., Shen, D., Yap, P.T.: Tract dictionary learning for fast and robust recognition of fiber bundles. In: Martel, A.L., Abolmaesumi, P., Stoyanov, D., Mateus, D., Zuluaga, M.A., Zhou, S.K., Racoceanu, D., Joskowicz, L. (eds.) Medical Image Computing and Computer Assisted Intervention – MICCAI 2020, pp. 251–259. Springer International Publishing, Cham (2020). https://doi.org/10.1007/978-3-030-59728-3_25
37. Kingma, D.P., Ba, J.: Adam: a method for stochastic optimization. arXiv preprint arXiv:1412.6980 (2017)
38. You, Y., Gitman, I., Ginsburg, B.: Large batch training of convolutional networks. arXiv preprint arXiv:1708.03888 (2017)
39. Tournier, J.D., et al.: MRtrix3: a fast, flexible and open software framework for medical image processing and visualisation. Neuroimage **202**, 116137 (2019)

40. Hochreiter, S., Schmidhuber, J.: Long short-term memory. Neural Comput. **9**(8), 1735–1780 (1997)
41. Sak, H., Senior, A., Beaufays, F.: Long Short-Term Memory Based Recurrent Neural Network Architectures for Large Vocabulary Speech Recognition. arXiv preprint arXiv:1402.1128 (2014)

Streamline Density Normalization: A Robust Approach to Mitigate Bundle Variability in Multi-site Diffusion MRI

Yixue Feng[✉], Yuhan Shuai, Julio E. Villalón-Reina, Bramsh Q. Chandio, Sophia I. Thomopoulos, Talia M. Nir, Neda Jahanshad, and Paul M. Thompson

Imaging Genetics Center, Stevens Neuroimaging and Informatics Institute, Keck School of Medicine, University of Southern California, Marina del Rey, CA, USA
yixuefen@usc.edu

Abstract. Tractometry enables quantitative analysis of tissue microstructure is sensitive to variability introduced during tractography and bundle segmentation. Differences in processing parameters and bundle geometry can lead to inconsistent streamline reconstructions and sampling, ultimately affecting the reproducibility of tractometry analysis. In this study, we introduce Streamline Density Normalization (SDNorm), a supervised two-step method designed to reduce variability in bundle reconstructions. SDNorm first computes streamline weights using linear regression to match a subject's bundle to a template streamline density map, then iteratively prunes streamlines to achieve a target density using a novel metric called *effective Streamline Point Density* (eSPD). We evaluate SDNorm across multiple bundles and acquisition protocols in dMRI data from a subset of subjects from Alzheimer's Disease Neuroimaging Initiative and demonstrate that it can significantly reduce variability in streamline density, improve consistency in along-tract microstructure profiles, and provide useful metrics for automated bundle quality control. These results suggest that SDNorm can help enhance the reproducibility and robustness of bundle reconstruction across heterogeneous image acquisition protocols and tractography settings, making it well-suited for large-scale and multi-site neuroimaging studies.

Keywords: tractography · bundle segmentation · tractometry

1   Introduction

Tractometry is an approach that map scalar microstructural measures along the brain's white matter (WM) fiber bundles, which can be identified by tractography. Tractometry analysis heavily depends on the consistency and accuracy of tractography and bundle segmentation. However, both steps suffer from high

© The Author(s), under exclusive license to Springer Nature Switzerland AG 2026
M. Chamberland et al. (Eds.): CDMRI 2025, LNCS 16205, pp. 44–56, 2026.
https://doi.org/10.1007/978-3-032-12837-9_5

variability across subjects, anatomical bundles, and diffusion MRI (dMRI) acquisitions.

Tractography requires the selection of numerous parameters—such as step size, seeding strategy, angle threshold and stopping criteria—whose optimal values may differ across studies. Bundle segmentation methods also rely on modifiable parameters such as distance thresholds, inclusion/exclusion criteria for ROI definitions, and atlas alignment. Even when processing parameters are held constant, anatomical differences across individuals and variability in data quality can affect the ability to reconstruct bundles of interest [16]. The inconsistency in these processing parameters directly impacts how scalar maps are sampled and interpolated in tractometry analyses. For example, regions with low streamline density may produce noisier tract profiles. This variability in streamline representation can complicate group-level comparisons, which typically do not account for differences in spatial sampling. Therefore, reducing arbitrary sources of variability in tractography and bundle segmentation is essential, to improve the reliability and reproducibility of tractometry studies.

A common class of streamline filtering methods focuses on improving the biological validity of tractography by aligning streamlines with the underlying diffusion signals or estimated fiber orientation distributions. Notable examples include Spherical-Deconvolution Informed Filtering of Tractograms (SIFT and SIFT2) [18,19], Convex Optimization Modeling of Microstructure Informed Tractograpy (COMMIT) [4], and Linear Fascicle Evaluation (LiFE) [13]. These supervised filtering methods are primarily designed for whole-brain tractograms in the context of connectivity analysis. However, they are not applicable to individual white matter (WM) bundles, as multiple tracts often intersect within the same voxel, or even fixel [17] at the current spatial resolution of diffusion MRI. In contrast, bundle-specific filtering methods —such as FiberNeat [3] and BundleCleaner [5]—remove anatomically implausible streamlines from bundles in an unsupervised approach, as a form of quality control. They assume coherent streamline trajectories and use clustering algorithms to remove streamlines. While these methods are effective when a bundle is overestimated—i.e., adequately reconstructed but contains false positive streamlines, they have limited use when a bundle is underestimated—i.e., has sparse streamlines and fails to capture the bundle's full spatial extent. This asymmetry in handling false positives and false negatives presents a key challenge for bundle-level quality control. Applying filtering indiscriminately to all extracted bundles may discard valid but sparse reconstructed fibers. Ideally, a robust approach should identify underestimated bundles while selectively filtering only overestimated bundles.

In this study, we introduce **Streamline Density Normalization (SDNorm)**, a two-step procedure that aims to reduce arbitrary sources of variability in extracted bundles across subjects and tractography settings. We propose to *normalize* the streamline density of bundles using a supervised approach instead of *filtering* to remove false positive streamlines. SDNorm first computes streamline weights to match an individual bundle to a template density map derived from a reference group using ridge regression. We also introduce a novel metric called **effective streamline point density (eSPD)** that describes the average number of streamline points traversing a unit voxel for a given bundle. In the second step of SDNorm, we iteratively prune each bundle based on streamline weights, until a target eSPD is reached. We assess SDNorm on multi-site diffusion MRI from the Alzheimer's Disease Neuroimaging Initiative (ADNI), and show that SDNorm can significantly reduce variability in streamline density and tractometry profiles across subjects and tractography settings. Moreover, metrics describing the model fit of the ridge regression model offer utility for automated QC and can help flag bundles that are underestimated or poorly constructed. Code for SDNorm is available at https://github.com/wendyfyx/SDNorm.

Table 1. ADNI3 participant characteristics by protocol (N=140). Protocol abbreviations are prefixed with the scanner vendor, where S stands for Siemens, P for Philips, and GE for General Electric. The number refers to the number of diffusion-weighted gradients. All protocols are single-shell with b=1000 s/mm^2, except for S127, that is multi-shell.

Protocol	Sex	Age	Diagnosis		
			CN	MCI	Dementia
GE36	10 M / 10 F	71.5 ± 6.8	10	9	1
GE54	10 M / 10 F	78.7 ± 7.7	10	7	3
P33	10 M / 10 F	76.8 ± 8.7	10	6	4
P36	10 M / 10 F	72.0 ± 7.0	10	9	1
S127	10 M / 10 F	72.7 ± 7.4	10	8	2
S31	10 M / 10 F	72.8 ± 7.5	10	9	1
S55	10 M / 10 F	75.7 ± 9.0	10	6	4

2   Data and Materials

2.1   Diffusion MRI Processing

To create the template density maps, we processed dMRI data from 200 sex-matched subjects (100 male / 100 female; 36–100 years old; mean age: 58.75 ± 14.86 (SD) years) from the Lifespan Human Connectome Project Aging (HCP-A) study [9] using processing steps described in [6]. All preprocessed DWI volumes have 1.5-mm isotropic voxel size. Fiber orientations were reconstructed using multi-shell multi-tissue constrained spherical deconvolution (msmtCSD) [10].

We analyzed DWI data from 140 participants from ADNI3 (**Table 1**) [24]. For each imaging protocol, we selected 20 subjects matched by sex. Within each protocol group, the cohort was further balanced by cognitive status, consisting of 10 cognitively normal (CN) individuals and 10 individuals diagnosed with either mild cognitive impairment (MCI) or dementia. Additional information on acquisition protocols and DWI preprocessing steps is available in [7] [21]. All DWI were resampled to 2-mm isotropic voxel size; fiber orientations were reconstructed using CSD [22] for single-shell diffusion protocols, except for S127, where msmtCSD was used.

2.2 Tractography Processing

For all HCP-A and ADNI3 subjects, we performed bundle-based tractography to extract 10 bundles - the arcuate fasciculus left (AF_L) and right (AF_R), cingulum frontal parietal left (C_FP_L) and right (C_FP_R), corpus callosum forceps major (CC_ForcepsMajor) and forceps minor (CC_ForcepsMinor), corticospinal tract left (CST_L) and right (CST_R), inferior fronto-occipital fasciculus left (IFOF_L) and right (IFOF_R). Inspired by Bundle-Specific Tractography [15] and Automatic Fiber Tracking from DSI-Studio [25], seeds were only set within the bundles of interest to constrain fiber tracking.

Atlas bundles were obtained from the population-averaged HCP-1065 Young Adult atlas [26]. To obtain the transform between the subject space and MNI space, a fractional anisotropy (FA) map was first computed for each ADNI3 subject by fitting DTI, and registered to the ICBM 2009a Nonlinear Asymmetric T1w template (1-mm isotropic voxel size) using ANTS Syn [23]. To create the seed mask, each atlas bundle was converted into a binary mask, dilated, and warped to the subject's dMRI space with the ANTS' non-linear transform. Eight seeds were randomly placed for each voxel within the seed mask. A binary stopping criterion was defined as the intersection of the dilated seed mask and FA > 0.05. We selected a relatively low FA threshold to ensure the streamlines are adequately reconstructed in regions with potentially reduced anisotropy due to neurodegeneration in ADNI3 subjects. For each of the 10 bundles of interest, local probabilistic tracking from DIPY [1,8] was used to generate streamlines with maximum angle of $20°$ and step size of 0.5 mm. Streamlines were retained if their lengths fell within the minimum and maximum range defined by the atlas bundle, with a 20% tolerance margin. After fiber tracking, the atlas bundles were warped to subject space and used to filter the generated streamlines with the Fast Streamline Search (FSS) algorithm [20]. FSS was chosen for its computational efficiency and simplicity, requiring only a single parameter —the search radius. We used a radius of 6 mm for all bundles, except for the IFOF, where a radius of 7 mm provided better segmentation results.

To evaluate the performance of SDNorm across tractography settings in ADNI3 subjects, we ran bundle-based tractography with the following modification to the parameters: the number of seeds per voxel was increased to 12, and the step size was decreased to 0.2 mm. We refer to this configuration as *Run B*, while the initial configuration with 8 seeds and 0.5 mm step size is referred to as *Run A*.

All bundles from all subjects and runs were manually quality-checked (QC) and labeled as "Pass," "Poor," or "Fail" based on their anatomical plausibility and streamline coverage. Bundles labeled "Poor" typically have limited coverage or contain visible false positives but could still be usable with additional processing. "Fail" labels were assigned to bundles with severe reconstruction issues—such as very few streamlines, large gaps, or anatomically implausible trajectories. All bundles from HCP-A subjects passed QC for template creation. Details for ADNI3 bundle QC are in **Section** 4.1.

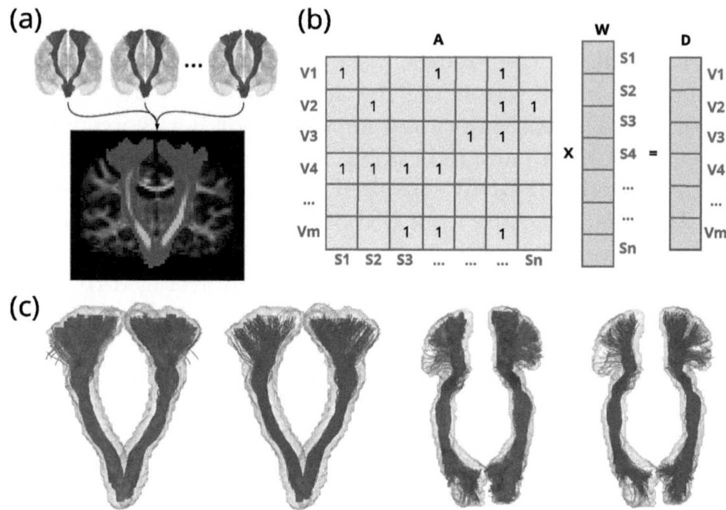

Fig. 1. Streamline Density Normalization (SDNorm). (a) Creating the group-level streamline density map of the corticospinal tract (CST) from a reference group. (b) SDNorm Step 1: Calculating streamline weights. c Examples bundles before and after SDNorm Step 2 pruning. *red*: streamlines discarded; *blue*: remaining streamlines.

3   Methods

In SDNorm, template density maps are first created for each bundle of interest from a reference group. Streamline weights are then calculated to match each subject bundle's density map to match the template, followed by a pruning procedure. We describe each step in detail below.

3.1   Template Map Creation

A density map is defined as the number of streamlines passing through voxels in a reference volume. Template density maps from 10 bundles of interest were computed from 200 HCP-A subjects (see Figure 1(a)). As the HCP pipeline produces processed dMRI in the MNI space, there was no need for registration to align density maps across subjects. For each bundle density map, voxels where only one streamline passes through were removed, and the map was normalized so that all values sum to 1. The normalized density maps were then averaged across subjects for each bundle. Gaussian smoothing ($\sigma = 0.5$) and log-filtering (voxels with the top 50% percentile log-density were retained) were then applied to the group average density map [11] to create the final template map.

3.2 SDNorm Step 1: Streamline Weight Calculation

The goal of this step is to assign one weight per streamline such that the weighted streamline density map for a given bundle best matches the corresponding template map, subject to regularization (see Figure 1(b)). We create the streamline-voxel adjacency matrix $A \in \mathbb{R}^{V \times S}$, where each column A_i is a binary vector indicating which voxels streamline i passes through, V is the number of voxels with non-zero streamline density in the reference volume, and S is the total number of streamlines in a given bundle. We compute weights $w \in \mathbb{R}^S$ with the following objective:

$$\min_{w \geq 0} \|\mu \cdot Aw - d\|_2^2 + \alpha \cdot \lambda \cdot \|w\|_2^2$$

where $d \in \mathbb{R}^V$ is the flattened template density map and λ is the ridge regularization weight. The first term matches streamline density map to the template, and the second term regularizes the weights to prevent overfitting. Inspired by the scaling parameters in SIFT2 [19], we defined μ, a fixed parameter to match the scale between streamline density and the normalized template map, and α, another fixed scaling parameter to control the effect of regularization as

$$\mu = \frac{\sum_{j=1}^{V} d}{\sum_{i=1}^{S} \sum_{j=1}^{V} A}, \qquad \alpha = \frac{1}{V} \sum_{j=1}^{V} d^2$$

Both μ and α are calculated prior to optimization, and w is the only free parameter.

3.3 SDNorm Step 2: Streamline Pruning

After the streamline weights w are computed, they can be used to weight streamline contributions in the second pruning procedure. Although the true underlying bundle-specific fiber density may differ, we aim to reduce inter-bundle density variability using the following pruning procedure: For a given bundle, we define the metric Streamline Point Density (SPD) as the total number of streamline points for a given bundle divided by the bundle volume. Suppose $\bar{L}$ is the average streamline length and c is the step size, both defined in millimeters (mm), the average number of points per streamline is $\frac{\bar{L}}{c}$. We can instead compute

$$\text{eSPD} = \frac{S \cdot \bar{L}}{\text{volume} \cdot c},$$

or **Effective Streamline Point Density (eSPD)**. This formulation makes it easier to prune streamlines: given a target eSPD, the number of streamlines to retain at iteration k is

$$S_k = \frac{\mathrm{eSPD}_{\mathrm{target}} \cdot \mathrm{volume}_{k-1} \cdot c}{\bar{L}_{k-1}}$$

At each iteration, S_k streamlines with the highest weights in w are retained, and volume and $\bar{L}$ are recomputed. We iteratively prune the bundle using this procedure until the desired eSPD is reached.

3.4   Experiments

In this study, we applied SDNorm to both run A and B bundles from 140 ADNI3 subjects. For each bundle, the corresponding template map is first warped to the subject space using the ANTS transform computed in **Section** 2.2. Due to difference in resolution between the template maps (1-mm isotropic) and subject space FA (2-mm isotropic), SDNorm step 1 is much faster when A and d are defined in the subject space. All subject bundles from run B are resampled to $s = 0.5$ mm fixed step size to match run A. SDNorm pruning was applied with a target eSPD of 8. For bundles with more than 10,000 streamlines, QuickBundles was used to downsample bundles to following the approach in BundleCleaner [5], and speed up model fitting in SDNorm step 1.

To evaluate the effect of SDNorm on along-tract profiles, we computed mean FA profiles for each bundle using Bundle Analytics (BUAN) [2]. BUAN creates 100 along-tract segments, and the FA values projected on streamline points within each segment are averaged to create the mean FA profile.

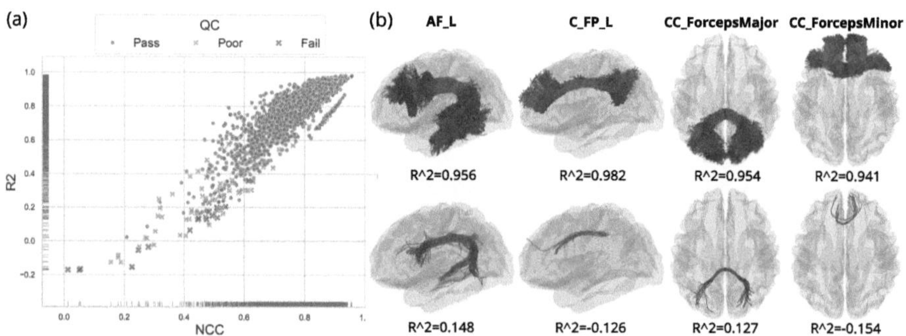

Fig. 2. Quality Control (QC) using SDNorm. (a) Normalized Cross Correlation (NCC) between the subjects' density maps and template map is plotted against R^2 from SDNorm Step 1, colored by QC labels. **(b)** Subject bundles with the highest and lowest R^2 across 4 bundles.

4 Results

4.1 Model Fit & Quality Control

After calculating streamline weights in SDNorm step 1, we evaluate model fit using R^2, the coefficient of determination. The average R^2 values for bundles from run A and run B were 0.79 ± 0.16 and 0.78 ± 0.17 respectively. We show bundles with the highest and lowest R^2 scores for 4 bundles in Fig. 2(b). Bundles with high R^2 are more densely packed and have good streamline coverage, whereas bundles with low R^2 are typically underestimated or contain streamlines with anatomically implausible trajectories. As R^2 is a metric describing the fit between a weighted streamline density map and the template map, we also calculate the normalized cross correlation (NCC) between the original unweighted streamline density map and the template map. We plot R^2 against NCC in Fig. 2(a), colored by labels from manual QC. Bundles labeled either"Poor" or "Fail" are concentrated in the lower left quadrant. Using thresholds of $R^2 = 0.4$ or $NCC = 0.5$ can well distinguish bundles that are labeled "Pass" (with precision of 0.985 and 0.983, and recall of 0.991 and 0.989 respectively) and both metrics show promise in automated bundle QC.

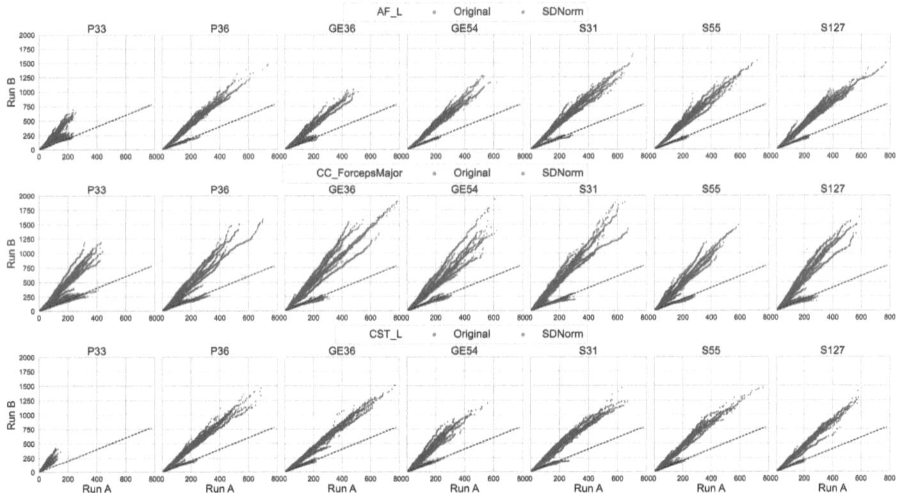

Fig. 3. Quantile-Quantile (Q-Q) Plot of density maps values from Run A bundles again those from Run B bundles before and after applying SDNorm, stratified by acquisition protocol across 3 bundles.

4.2 Evaluation on Streamline Density

To evaluate the effectiveness of SDNorm in reducing variability across tractography settings, we compared the streamline density distributions between Run

A and Run B using Quantile-Quantile (Q-Q) plots for all ADNI3 subjects, stratified by acquisition protocol. Results for three representative bundles are shown in Fig. 3. The black dashed line represents the reference distribution where both runs have identical density distributions. Prior to SDNorm, the Q-Q plots for the original bundles (red) exhibit consistently steep slopes, indicating that Run B bundles have substantially higher streamline densities than Run A—a result expected due to the increased seeding density used in Run B. After applying SDNorm, the Q-Q plots (blue) align much more closely with the reference line, indicating that the density distribution are much more similar between two runs. Aside from the change in slopes in the Q-Q plots, SDNorm also suppresses extreme values in the density distribution. For instance, peak densities reached nearly 2,000 streamlines per voxel in some CC_ForcepsMajor bundles before SDNorm, whereas peak density values were consistently reduced to below 300 streamlines per voxel after SDNorm.

We also observed moderate variability in streamline density across different bundles and acquisition protocols. Prior to SDNorm, CC_ForcepsMajor exhibited both higher peak densities and greater inter-subject variability compared to AF_L and CST_L. Protocol P33, in particular, yielded bundles with lower peak density than other protocols across bundles. CST_L bundles from P33 peak below 400 streamlines per voxel, and they likely had low eSPD values and were therefore not subject to pruning. Overall, these results demonstrate that SDNorm effectively reduces variability in streamline density across tractography settings, subjects and protocols.

4.3   Along-Tract Profile of Fractional Anisotropy

We further evaluated the impact of SDNorm on along-tract FA profiles by evaluating the similarity of profiles between Run A and Run B. For each bundle, we computed the L2 norm between the mean FA profiles from two runs, defined as $FA_{diff} = \|FA_A - FA_B\|_2$, where FA_A and FA_B are the mean FA profiles defined along 100 segments for run A and B, as detailed in **Section** 3.4.

Since bundles from both runs are derived from the same diffusion data and the same FA map is sampled, we expect their mean FA profiles to be similar. However, differences in streamline geometry and density between the two tractography settings can introduce variability in how the scalar values are sampled and interpolated. To assess whether SDNorm reduces this variability, we performed a paired statistical analysis using the Wilcoxon signed-rank test, testing the hypothesis that FA_{diff} is significantly lower after SDNorm. Figure 4 shows boxplots of FA_{diff} for all 10 bundles before and after applying SDNorm, along with the p-values from the Wilcoxon test. Across all bundles, the differences in mean FA profiles between Run A and Run B were significantly reduced following SDNorm ($p < 0.05$, FDR corrected), indicating improved consistency in FA profiles. Among the bundles evaluated, CC_ForcepsMajor exhibited the largest FA_{diff} values and the greatest inter-subject variance, both before and after SDNorm. This is consistent with their higher streamline density and geometric variability observed in earlier analyses.

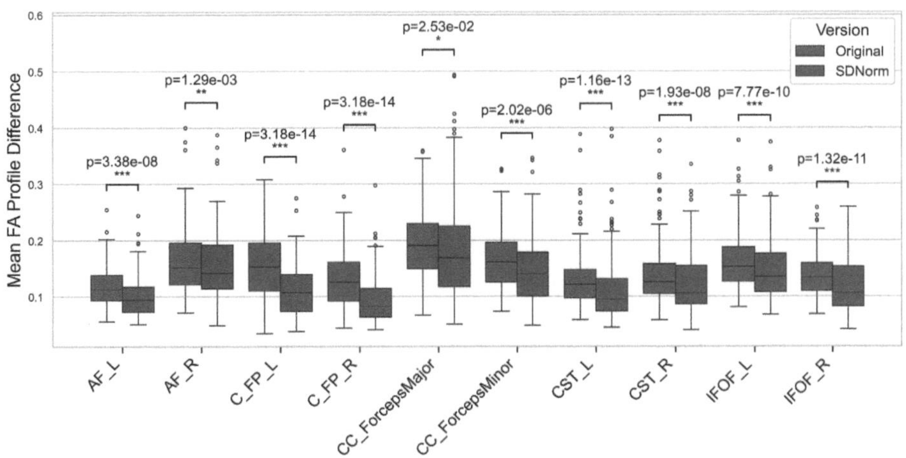

Fig. 4. Boxplots of $\mathrm{FA_{diff}}$ **before and after applying SDNorm across 10 bundles.** Significance levels and FDR-corrected p-values from the Wilcoxon test is shown for each bundles (*: $p < 0.05$, **: $p < 0.01$, ***: $p < 0.001$).

These findings indicated that SDNorm leads to more stable and reproducible along-tract microstructural profiles, which is essential for downstream group analyses and clinical interpretation.

5   Discussion

In this study, we introduced SDNorm, a supervised method for normalizing bundle streamline density across tractography settings and subjects. SDNorm is a two step procedure, and contains only 3 user-defined parameters—step size, regularization weight, and target eSPD.

A potential concern is that SDNorm may reduce subject-level variability when matching subject bundles to a template map. Importantly, SDNorm does not "upsample" bundles with streamline densities below the target eSPD threshold, thereby preserving sparse reconstructions that may reflect biological variability. Users may select higher eSPD thresholds to retain more subject variability and lower thresholds to apply stricter density normalization. In tractometry applications, statistical stability of microstructural profiles can vary across datasets and bundles of interest, as their values depend on acquisition protocols [14]. In this study, we have shown that FA profiles are more reproducible across tractography settings after applying SDNorm. In future work, we aim to systematically investigate how different pruning thresholds may influence the stability of along-tract microstructural measures and the detection of biologically meaningful variability across subjects.

An important consideration when using SDNorm is the choice of template density maps. We recommend that users generate a study-specific template map using a subset of their study cohort or a demographically matched reference group processed with similar bundle extraction pipelines. To support this, we provide code for constructing the template maps in the SDNorm Github repository.

Lastly, we note that SDNorm was developed and evaluated using bundles generated with probabilistic tractography. Deterministic tractography is less sensitive to uncertainty in fiber orientations and tends to generate streamlines that are more densely packed in the core of WM bundles, while probabilistic tractography tends to produce a wider spread of streamlines [12]. Due to such differences, we do not recommend using templates generated from deterministic tractography when normalizing bundles from probabilistic tractography, or *vice versa*. Future work will investigate how SDNorm performs on deterministic tractography.

6   Conclusion

We propose SDNorm, a supervised method for reducing bundle variability by normalizing streamline density. By incorporating a model fitting step and the novel resolution-independent eSPD metric in pruning, SDNorm requires three intuitive user-defined parameters and can be applied to different anatomical bundles. Applied to multi-site data from ADNI3, we show that SDNorm can reduce differences in streamline density distribution across subjects and tractography settings and improve the reproducibility of along-tract FA profiles. In addition, model fit metrics derived from SDNorm can assist with automated quality control by identifying poorly reconstructed bundles. This approach offers a practical and scalable solution for improving the reliability of bundle extraction and tractometry in studies with multi-site dMRI data.

Acknowledgments. This study was supported by the National Institute on Aging (NIA) under grant RF1-NS136995, the National Institute of Health (NIH) under grant NIH-T32AG058507, National Institute of Mental Health under grant R01MH134004 and the US Alzheimer's Association under grant AARG-23-1149996.

Disclosure of Interests. The authors have no competing interests to declare that are relevant to the content of this article

References

1. Behrens, T., et al.: Characterization and propagation of uncertainty in diffusion-weighted MR imaging. Magn. Reson. Med. **50**(5), 1077–1088 (2003). https://doi.org/10.1002/mrm.10609
2. Chandio, B.Q., et al.: Bundle analytics, a computational framework for investigating the shapes and profiles of brain pathways across populations. Sci. Rep. **10**(1), 17149 (2020). https://doi.org/10.1038/s41598-020-74054-4
3. Chandio, B.Q., et al.: FiberNeat: unsupervised streamline clustering and white matter tract filtering in latent space. preprint, Neuroscience (Oct 2021). https://doi.org/10.1101/2021.10.26.465991

4. Daducci, A., et al.: COMMIT: convex optimization modeling for microstructure informed tractography. IEEE Trans. Med. Imaging **34**(1), 246–257 (2015). https://doi.org/10.1109/TMI.2014.2352414

5. Feng, Y., et al.: BundleCleaner: unsupervised denoising and subsampling of diffusion MRI-derived tractography data. In: Computational Diffusion MRI, vol. 14328, pp. 152–164. Springer Nature Switzerland, Cham (2023). https://doi.org/10.1007/978-3-031-47292-3_14

6. Feng, Y., et al.: BundleAGE: predicting white matter age using along-tract microstructural profiles from diffusion MRI. In: 2024 20th International Symposium on Medical Information Processing and Analysis (SIPAIM), IEEE, Antigua, Guatemala (2024). https://doi.org/10.1109/SIPAIM62974.2024.10783507

7. Feng, Y., et al.: Microstructural mapping of neural pathways in Alzheimer's disease using macrostructure-informed normative tractometry. Alzheimer's & Dementia p. alz.14371 (2024). https://doi.org/10.1002/alz.14371

8. Garyfallidis, E., et al.: Dipy, a library for the analysis of diffusion MRI data. Front. Neuroinformatics **8** (2014). https://doi.org/10.3389/fninf.2014.00008

9. Harms, M.P., et al.: Extending the human connectome project across ages: imaging protocols for the lifespan development and aging projects. Neuroimage **183**, 972–984 (2018). https://doi.org/10.1016/j.neuroimage.2018.09.060

10. Jeurissen, B., et al.: Multi-tissue constrained spherical deconvolution for improved analysis of multi-shell diffusion MRI data. Neuroimage **103**, 411–426 (2014). https://doi.org/10.1016/j.neuroimage.2014.07.061

11. Maffei, C., et al.: Insights from the IronTract challenge: optimal methods for mapping brain pathways from multi-shell diffusion MRI. Neuroimage **257**, 119327 (2022). https://doi.org/10.1016/j.neuroimage.2022.119327

12. Maier-Hein, K.H., et al.: The challenge of mapping the human connectome based on diffusion tractography. Nat. Commun. **8**(1), 1349 (2017). https://doi.org/10.1038/s41467-017-01285-x

13. Pestilli, F., et al.: Evaluation and statistical inference for human connectomes. Nat. Methods **11**(10), 1058–1063 (2014). https://doi.org/10.1038/nmeth.3098. number: 10 Publisher: Nature Publishing Group

14. Reid, L.B., Cespedes, M.I., Pannek, K.: How many streamlines are required for reliable probabilistic tractography? Solutions for microstructural measurements and neurosurgical planning. Neuroimage **211**, 116646 (2020). https://doi.org/10.1016/j.neuroimage.2020.116646

15. Rheault, F., et al.: Bundle-specific tractography with incorporated anatomical and orientational priors. Neuroimage **186**, 382–398 (2019). https://doi.org/10.1016/j.neuroimage.2018.11.018

16. Schilling, K.G., et al.: Fiber tractography bundle segmentation depends on scanner effects, vendor effects, acquisition resolution, diffusion sampling scheme, diffusion sensitization, and bundle segmentation workflow. Neuroimage **242**, 118451 (2021). https://doi.org/10.1016/j.neuroimage.2021.118451

17. Schilling, K.G., et al.: Prevalence of white matter pathways coming into a single white matter voxel orientation: the bottleneck issue in tractography. Hum. Brain Mapp. **43**(4), 1196–1213 (2022). https://doi.org/10.1002/hbm.25697

18. Smith, R.E., et al.: SIFT: spherical-deconvolution informed filtering of tractograms. Neuroimage **67**, 298–312 (2013). https://doi.org/10.1016/j.neuroimage.2012.11.049

19. Smith, R.E., et al.: SIFT2: enabling dense quantitative assessment of brain white matter connectivity using streamlines tractography. Neuroimage **119**, 338–351 (2015). https://doi.org/10.1016/j.neuroimage.2015.06.092

20. St-Onge, E., et al.: Fast streamline search: an exact technique for diffusion MRI tractography. Neuroinformatics **20**(4), 1093–1104 (2022). https://doi.org/10.1007/s12021-022-09590-7
21. Thomopoulos, S.I., et al.: Diffusion MRI metrics and their relation to dementia severity: effects of harmonization approaches. In: 17th International Symposium on Medical Information Processing and Analysis, pp. 79. SPIE, Campinas, Brazil (2021). https://doi.org/10.1117/12.2606337
22. Tournier, J.D., et al.: Robust determination of the fibre orientation distribution in diffusion MRI: non-negativity constrained super-resolved spherical deconvolution. Neuroimage **35**(4), 1459–1472 (2007). https://doi.org/10.1016/j.neuroimage.2007.02.016
23. Tustison, N.J., et al.: The ANTsX ecosystem for quantitative biological and medical imaging. Sci. Rep. **11**(1), 9068 (2021). https://doi.org/10.1038/s41598-021-87564-6
24. Weiner, M.W., et al.: The Alzheimer's disease neuroimaging initiative 3: continued innovation for clinical trial improvement. Alzheimer's Dement. J. Alzheimer's Assoc. **13**(5), 561–571 (2017). https://doi.org/10.1016/j.jalz.2016.10.006
25. Yeh, F.C.: Shape analysis of the human association pathways. Neuroimage **223**, 117329 (2020). https://doi.org/10.1016/j.neuroimage.2020.117329
26. Yeh, F.C.: Population-based tract-to-region connectome of the human brain and its hierarchical topology. Nat. Commun. **13**(1), 4933 (2022). https://doi.org/10.1038/s41467-022-32595-4

Quantifying Parameter Estimation Difficulty of dMRI Models by Submanifold Geometry in Signal Space

Yoshitaka Masutani[(✉)], Kousei Konya, and Yuki Ichinoseki

Tohoku University Graduate School of Medicine, Sendai, Miyagi, Japan
`yoshitaka.masutani.a8@tohoku.ac.jp`

Abstract. Parametric models of diffusion MRI (dMRI) are extensively employed in both research and clinical contexts. These models yield parameters that characterize the local microstructural properties of biological tissues, derived through model fitting to real data. However, obtaining reliable parameter estimates remains challenging, primarily due to the influence of measurement noise. While several pioneering studies have addressed this issue by quantifying estimation uncertainty using bootstrap-based approaches, the present study shifts focus to the intrinsic characteristics of the models themselves, independent of measurement noise. To this end, we propose three novel metrics based on the geometry of the submanifold defined by the dMRI model within the signal space. For the models of diffusional kurtosis imaging (DKI) and neurite orientation dispersion and density imaging (NODDI), these metrics were evaluated at the typical parameter sets of brain tissues. The outcomes align with established insights in dMRI parameter estimation and suggest that the proposed metrics hold promise as new criteria for assessing the reliability of dMRI parameters.

Keywords: dMRI models · parameter estimation · submanifold

1 Introduction

Parametric models of diffusion MRI (dMRI) have been extensively applied in both research and clinical settings, with a diverse array of models developed to date, including the widely adopted diffusion tensor imaging (DTI) model [1]. Among these, the DTI model remains one of the most popular, particularly in the investigation of neurological pathologies such as stroke [2], cerebral infarction [3], and brain tumors [4]. The conceptual foundation of parametric modeling traces back to the seminal work of Stejskal and Tanner, who introduced an early framework within MR spectroscopy aimed at estimating the diffusion coefficient alone [5]. Subsequently, more sophisticated models have emerged to characterize non-Gaussian diffusion behavior [6] and to account for perfusion-related signal contributions [7], offering deeper insights into the underlying tissue microstructure.

Furthermore, several advanced models have been designed to directly quantify specific microstructural features, including axonal diameter [8], neurite orientation dispersion [9], soma size [10], and inter-compartmental water exchange [11]. Those parameters are obtained based on model fitting to real diffusion-weighted imaging (DWI) data. It is often hard to obtain robust estimation of parameters due to mixture of influence by several factors mainly by noise in image measurement. To improve the quality of estimated parameters, various approaches have been introduced including motion probing gradient (MPG) optimization, denoising and estimation by machine learning (ML). In addition, quantification of such estimation difficulty has been also investigated. In general, assessing the quality of parameter estimation using real data is inherently challenging due to the absence of a definitive ground truth for parameter values. As an alternative, uncertainty quantification based on the bootstrap method has been proposed [12,13], providing a practical means to evaluate parameter variability under specific measurement conditions. However, the metric is thought to be influenced by mixture of signal model property, measurement setting and noise. Measurement noise is widely recognized as a primary contributor to estimation errors and challenges. Moreover, the number of acquired measurements significantly influences model fitting performance. In addition to these factors, the intrinsic properties of the models themselves also play a critical role, exerting a notable impact on the accuracy and reliability of parameter estimation. More concretely, estimation difficulty can be different among parameter values, independently of noise. Therefore, it is important to reveal parameter-local characteristics of models. Such an investigation into dMRI models is anticipated to enhance the quality of parameter estimation. For instance, ML-based approaches to parameter estimation may benefit from these findings, as they offer valuable insights for the design and optimization of training datasets.

Based on the geometric structure of the submanifold defined by a model within the signal space, this study presents preliminary findings derived from three novel metrics proposed within our framework, each reflecting the parameter estimation difficulty. These metrics were evaluated using representative parameter sets corresponding to typical brain normal and abnormal tissues, employing the diffusional kurtosis imaging (DKI) model [6] and the neurite orientation dispersion and density imaging (NODDI) model [9].

2   Methods

2.1   dMRI Model as Submanifold in Signal Space

For generalization, we assume a dMRI signal model with M parameters; $\mathbf{p} = (p_1, ..., p_M) \in \mathbb{R}^M$ where each component p_i has a certain value range: $min_{p_i} - max_{p_i}$. A subset of $\mathbf{p}$ may form vector or tensor such as those in 3D models such as DTI and NODDI. Some parameters are mathematically bounded, as in the example of the NODDI model where the orientation dispersion (OD) parameter ranges from 0.0 to 1.0, while others have bio-physical bounds. For example, diffusivity-related parameters such as diffusion coefficient have only positive values but its upper bound is not mathematically given. Instead, we can consider a bio-physical upper bound. It is known that the value of diffusion coefficient of free water is around $3.0 \times 10^{-3}\ mm^2/s$. However, the values of apparent diffusion coefficient (ADC) in the brain show higher values due to mixture of faster component such as perfusion or bulk flow in the CSF [14]. Therefore, we can use $6.0 \sim 10.0 \times 10^{-3}\ mm^2/s$ for example. Then N DWI images are acquired to be performed with b-vectors: $\mathbf{b}_1, ..., \mathbf{b}_N$, i.e. unit vectors of MPG direction multiplied by b-values in the Pulse Gradient Spin Echo (PGSE) scheme. Here, the signal model is expressed as $S = S(\mathbf{p}, \mathbf{b})$. Basically, measurement is performed with $N \geq M$, often $N \gg M$ for obtaining reliable estimation against noise. Next, N-dimensional signal space is defined, in which a point $\mathbf{s} = (s_1, ..., s_N) \in \mathbb{R}^N$ represents a combination of signal values by N measurements for a single voxel location. In the space, a dMRI signal model $S = S(\mathbf{p}, \mathbf{b})$ forms a M-dimensional submanifold $\mathcal{M}$ which is bounded within the limited parameter ranges defined above. At an arbitrary point $\mathbf{S}$ on $\mathcal{M}$, a set of N signal values must satisfy model equation, that is, $\mathbf{S}(\mathbf{p}) = (S(\mathbf{p}, \mathbf{b}_1), ..., S(\mathbf{p}, \mathbf{b}_N)) \in \mathbb{R}^N$. Alternatively, we can use signal attenuation, that is, a signal value normalized by a baseline value S_0 both for the model and measurements.

In this scheme, parameter estimation is a search of a point $\hat{\mathbf{p}}$ on $\mathcal{M}$ as an optimal parameter set for a given point $\mathbf{s}$ of measurement signals (mostly away from $\mathcal{M}$) as shown in Fig. 1a. For the search, distance d between the two points $\mathbf{s}$ and $S(\hat{\mathbf{p}})$ is often minimized [15] by least squared fitting and so on with or without constraints of parameter ranges. Here, against a measurement point $\mathbf{s}$, we assume noiseless (or ideal) signal point $\check{\mathbf{s}}$ which is not necessarily on the submanifold as shown in Fig. 1a. Because every model is just approximation, we can hardly know such point. Instead, we use signal point $\mathbf{S}$ on $\mathcal{M}$ which perfectly follow the signal model equation. If a model reflects the signal formation process well, $\check{\mathbf{s}}$ is expected to be close to $\mathcal{M}$, and the closest point $S(\hat{\mathbf{p}})$ to $\check{\mathbf{s}}$ can be virtually defined as the signal points of the parameter set $\hat{\mathbf{p}}$ to be estimated. The location difference between $\mathbf{s}$ and $\check{\mathbf{s}}$ corresponds to measurement noise. In numerical solutions, initial estimation $\mathbf{p}_{init}$ on $\mathcal{M}$ is given first, then it is moved to a closer location to $\mathbf{s}$ iteratively with restriction on $\mathcal{M}$. The search can be trapped at local minima of the distance depending on local geometry of the submanifold in addition to location of $\mathbf{p}_{init}$. In the next section, such submanifold geometry is quantified for judging parameter estimation difficulty.

2.2 Metrics for Parameter Estimation Difficulty

The main objective of this study is to quantify estimation difficulty at a specific parameter set $\hat{\mathbf{p}}$ depending on locations of $\hat{\mathbf{p}}$ on $\mathcal{M}$ as local characteristics of submanifold and without influence of measurement noise. We define $\hat{\mathbf{p}}$ as parameters-of-interest (POI) to be an estimation target. For that purpose, various metrics such as higher order curvature around $\hat{\mathbf{p}}$ on the submanifold can be considered. For simplicity in this preliminary study, however, we determined to begin with 1D submanifold corresponding to each single parameter. For the i-th parameter, a 1D submanifold $\mathcal{M}_i(\hat{\mathbf{p}})$ is defined as an arc, which is a subset of $\mathcal{M}$ (Fig. 1b). As summarized in the examples in Fig. 2, simple geometry of the arcs can influence the parameter estimation so that three metrics are defined and used in this study as the followings.

1) *Length of single parameter arc*: This metric shows the total length of the arc with dimensionality correction factor of $\sqrt{N}$ passing through POI $\hat{\mathbf{p}}$ for each parameter and is defined as $L_p(\hat{\mathbf{p}}) = \int_{min_p}^{max_p} \|\mathbf{dS}\|/\sqrt{N}$. This metric influences parameter estimation in two principal aspects. First, a shorter range may induce out-of-range errors, as illustrated in Fig. 2a. When an estimation scheme constrains the output by rounding values within predefined bounds, such errors may become concealed, yet the frequency of rounded values increases noticeably. Additionally, the arc length within the signal space directly reflects sensitivity to noise, that is, shorter arcs are associated with greater susceptibility, thereby rendering parameter estimation more challenging, as demonstrated in the DKI results (see Fig. 3).

2) *Local curvature radius of single parameter arc*: By curvature κ computed at POI $\hat{\mathbf{p}}$ by derivative of unit tangent vector $\mathbf{t}_p$ on the arc, radius of curvature with dimensionality correction $R_p(\hat{\mathbf{p}}) = \kappa^{-1}/\sqrt{N}$ is obtained. This metric is considered to reflect the likelihood of estimation errors with dependency on magnitude of noise. As depicted in Fig. 2b, elevated curvature combined with a non-negligible level of noise may lead to erroneous minimization of the distance between the measurement point and the submanifold. Consequently, this results in larger estimation errors compared to scenarios involving lower curvature.

3) *Correlation factor of a parameter pair*: This metric quantifies relation of two parameters p_i and p_j by dot product of the pair of unit tangent vectors at POI $\hat{\mathbf{p}}$ and is defined as $C_{p_i,p_j}(\hat{\mathbf{p}}) = \mathbf{t}_{p_i}(\hat{\mathbf{p}}) \cdot \mathbf{t}_{p_j}(\hat{\mathbf{p}})$. Distinct from the other two metrics, this one captures the mutual dependency of estimation errors between two parameters. As shown in Fig. 2c, movement of measurement point parallel to the arc of p_i due to noise yield errors of the parameter p_i. Then, if p_j is strongly correlated to p_i, the error of p_j is larger than that of weaker correlation. The sign of this metric signifies the directional relationship between the errors of the two parameters- a positive value indicates that the errors share the same sign, whereas a negative value denotes opposing signs.

By using these metrics, the two models of DKI and NODDI were examined with typical measurement settings as described in the next section.

3   Results

DKI and NODDI are frequently employed for the quantitative characterization of brain tissues, including pathological structures. It is well established that distinct tissue types exhibit characteristic parameter values influenced by factors such as tissue composition, age, and disease severity. Accordingly, we evaluated the

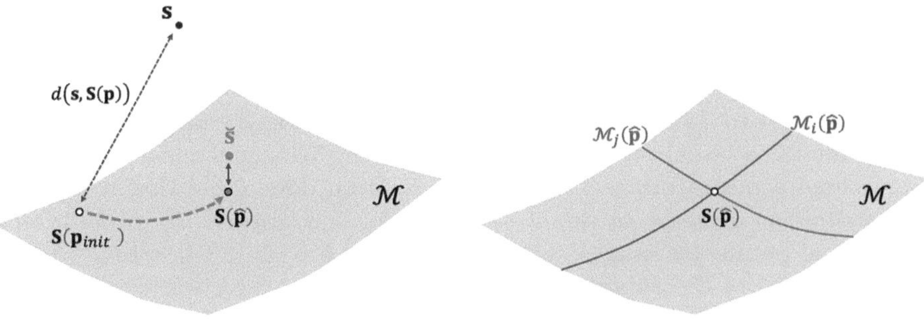

a) Parameter estimation equivalent to search of p̂ on M so that the distance $D(\mathbf{s}, \mathbf{S}(\mathbf{p}))$ is minimized. Note that noiseless signal point š may not be on M

b) To investigate local properties of M around p̂, 1D arc of as subset of submanifold M through p̂ for each parameter is employed.

Fig. 1. dMRI model as submanifold in signal space (ex. $N = 3, M = 2$). a) parameter search for measurements $\mathbf{s}$, b) $\mathcal{M}_i(\hat{\mathbf{p}})$ as 1D subset of $\mathcal{M}$ through the POI $\hat{\mathbf{p}}$.

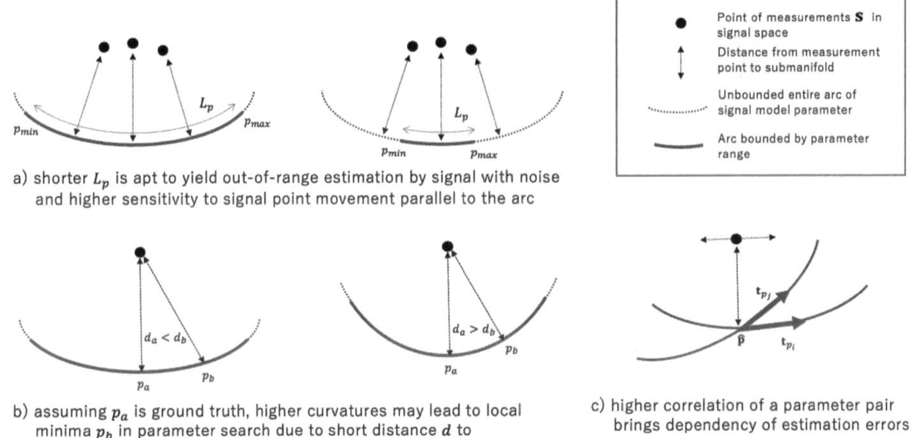

a) shorter L_p is apt to yield out-of-range estimation by signal with noise and higher sensitivity to signal point movement parallel to the arc

b) assuming p_a is ground truth, higher curvatures may lead to local minima p_b in parameter search due to short distance d to measurement point

c) higher correlation of a parameter pair brings dependency of estimation errors

Fig. 2. Three metrics reflecting parameter estimation difficulties and errors. a) arc length of single parameter, b) curvature of single parameter arc, and c) correlation factor of parameter pair.

proposed metrics at POIs corresponding to various tissue categories under representative MPG acquisition settings. In this study, we used signal decay ratio for the signal space by assuming that reliable S_0 is obtained by multiple b=0 DWI acquisitions. Derivatives and integrals are obtained by numerical computation with central difference approximation.

3.1   DKI Model Example

First, we examined 1D DKI model which has two parameters of diffusion coefficient D and diffusional kurtosis K. Measurements with $(1, 0, 0)$ of MPG vector with single b=0 acquisition and non-zero b-values of 311, 1244, and 2800 s/mm^2 are used. This simple example of $N = 3$ and $M = 2$ enables us to visualize the shape of the submanifold in 3D space. Note that signal space dimension is reduced from 4 to 3 by using signal decay ratio. In Fig. 3, the 2D submanifold of DKI model is visualized as a curved surface in 3D signal space, with points of measured signals from real brain data as green dots. Note that a constrain by monotonous decrease of signal $3/DK < b_{max}$ is applied [6] in addition to bio-physical parameter ranges of $0 \leq K \leq 4$ and $0 \leq D \leq 6.0 \times 10^{-3}$ mm^2/s. The thin shape of the submanifold has a longitudinal direction by D value so that with higher values of D, signal points move closer to the origin $(0, 0, 0)$. It is observed that the real measurement points are mostly distributed around the submanifold while some dots far from it are expected to yield large estimation errors.

Table 1 shows the computation results of the metrics at typical parameter values of D and K for several types of brain tissues including three categories of cerebral infarction, i.e. subacute lesions in the central and peripheral areas of the brain in addition to acute one [6,16,17]. As seen in the submanifold shape and the values of L_D,L_K,R_D and R_K, K estimation seems to be harder than that of D. This observation matches our general findings on the difficulty in DKI parameter estimation. More specifically, the small value of L_K for the core of subacute infarction (L_K=0.0013) means that K estimation for that type of tissue is quite hard. In addition, the negative values of $C(D, K)$ implies error correlation such as overestimation of D may induce underestimation of K.

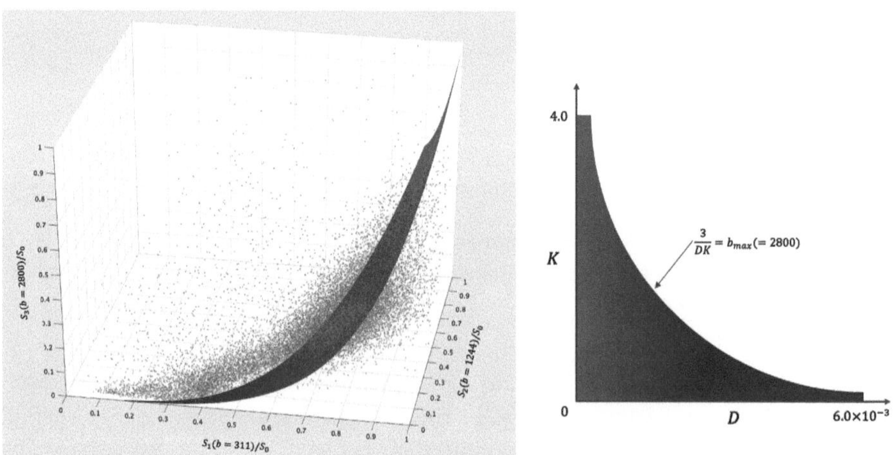

Fig. 3. Visualization of DKI submanifold in 3D space with measurement signal points as green dots (left). Note that parameters have constraint of positive values, bio-physical upper bounds, and inverse proportionality due to monotonical signal decrease by b-values determined in 2D parameter space (right). The colors for combinations of two parameters are common in the 3D visualization and the 2D map. (Color figure online)

Table 1. DKI metric values at typical parameter combinations in brain tissues.

Parameter set		D		K		$D-K$
tissue type	POI $(D{\times}10^3, K)$	L_D	R_D	L_K	R_K	$C_{D,K}$
WM (frontal)	(0.85,0.94)	1.1863	0.2108	0.2181	0.1827	−0.6295
WM (internal capsule)	(0.84,1.0)	1.1584	0.1840	0.2260	0.1926	−0.5953
GM next to CSF	(0.96,0.83)	1.2589	0.2267	0.2006	0.1532	−0.6185
GM next to WM	(0.84,0.65)	1.3177	0.3452	0.1852	0.1498	−0.7636
thalamus	(0.92,0.93)	1.2050	0.1860	0.2158	0.1727	−0.5723
putamen	(0.78,0.74)	1.2584	0.3320	0.1967	0.1706	−0.7615
subacute infarction (core)	(0.2,0.59)	0.7701	0.9597	0.0013	0.7079	−0.9691
subacute infarction (peripheral)	(0.46,1.60)	0.8551	0.1786	0.2420	0.3330	−0.7346
acute infarction	(0.59,0.61)	1.2534	0.4242	0.1873	0.2101	−0.8515

The parameter range of D (mm^2/s) is $0.0{\sim}\min(6.0{\times}10^{-3}, 3.0K^{-1}b_{max}{}^{-1})$, that of K is $0.0{\sim}\min(4.0, 3.0D^{-1}b_{max}{}^{-1})$.
The POI values on the list are determined by reference to [4] for WM, GM, thalamus and putamen, [16] for subacute infarction and [17] for acute infarction.

3.2   NODDI Model Example

For the NODDI model examination, we employed the three-shell MPG settings of Human Connectome Project (HCP) [18], which forms 270-dimensional space of normalized signal decay. The three metrics were computed for volume fraction of isotropic diffusion f_{iso}, and intracellular compartment f_{ic} and orientation dispersion OD with fixed vector of dispersion center $\mathbf{u}{=}(1,0,0)$.

First, around at the POI of $f_{iso} = f_{ic} = OD = 0.5$, metrics of three 1D arcs were examined (Fig. 4). Figure 4a shows changes of L and R metrics for f_{ic} and OD in the range of $f_{iso} : 0.0 \sim 1.0$ with other two parameters fixed at $f_{ic} = OD = 0.5$. Similarly, Fig. 4b and 4c display those of a single parameter change with fixed pairs of other two parameters. Then, the metrics were computed for various brain tissue types including glioma of three grades and two types [19,20] as shown in Table 2. In Fig. 4, it is interesting that higher f_{iso} and lower f_{ic} may cause harder estimation of those two parameters while difficulty of OD estimation seems almost equal in the whole range except for those lower than 0.2.

Then, the $R_{f_{iso}}$ values at the POI are exceptionally high, causing the corresponding plots to exceed the display range in the line graphs (Fig. 4b and 4c). This indicates that the curvature of the 1D submanifold corresponding to f_{iso} is exceedingly low, resulting in an almost linear trajectory within the signal space. Overall, the R values at the POI increase in the order of OD, f_{ic} and f_{iso}, indicating that the corresponding curvature values follow the inverse order. As explained above with Fig. 2b, higher curvature may cause more estimation error, and therefore NODDI parameter estimation around the POI may be hard in the order of OD, f_{ic} and f_{iso}. In addition, markedly negative values (< -0.94) of the correlation coefficient between f_{ic} and f_{iso} were observed in Table 2, indicating a strong inverse dependency in the estimation errors of these parameters.

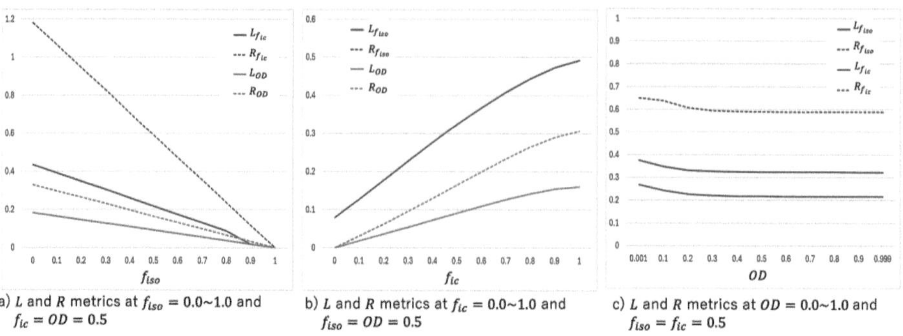

Fig. 4. Three metrics reflecting parameter estimation difficulties and errors. Note that $R_{f_{iso}}$ values in b) and c) are extremely high and out of the plot range.

Table 2. NODDI metric values at typical parameter combinations in brain tissues.

tissue type	POI (f_{iso}, f_{ic}, OD) with $\mathbf{u}=(1,0,0)$	$L_{f_{iso}}$	$R_{f_{iso}}$	$L_{f_{ic}}$	$R_{f_{ic}}$	L_{OD}	R_{OD}	$C_{f_{iso},f_{ic}}$	$C_{f_{ic},OD}$	$C_{OD,f_{iso}}$
	Parameter set		f_{iso}		f_{ic}		OD	$f_{iso} - f_{ic}$	$f_{ic} - OD$	$OD - f_{iso}$
WM	(0.09,0.55, 0.28)	0.3494	$> 10^{11}$	0.4022	0.9586	0.1823	0.3511	−0.9733	−0.2143	0.1602
GM	(0.11,0.38,0.34)	0.2677	$> 10^{11}$	0.3899	1.3803	0.1229	0.2366	−0.9744	−0.1563	0.1123
CSF	(0.66,0.17,0.07)	0.1690	$> 10^{11}$	0.1695	0.8869	0.0208	0.0127	−0.9426	−0.4544	0.2793
glioma G2 T2L	(0.36,0.15,0.46)	0.1520	$> 10^{11}$	0.2780	1.5810	0.0345	0.0611	−0.9511	−0.0957	0.0513
glioma G3 T2L	(0.43,0.11,0.42)	0.1319	$> 10^{11}$	0.2481	1.5278	0.0225	0.0406	−0.9374	−0.1087	0.0499
glioma G4 T2L	(0.35,0.19,0.39)	0.1723	$> 10^{11}$	0.2835	1.4859	0.0445	0.0823	−0.9594	−0.1228	0.0725
glioma G2 CEL	(0.15,0.30,0.44)	0.2274	$> 10^{11}$	0.3696	1.5517	0.0924	0.1678	−0.9716	−0.1063	0.0727
glioma G3 CEL	(0.41,0.24,0.34)	0.1979	$> 10^{11}$	0.2585	1.2228	0.0512	0.0975	−0.9662	−0.1494	0.0958
glioma G4 CEL	(0.10,0.35,0.47)	0.2520	$> 10^{11}$	0.3908	1.4799	0.1144	0.2054	−0.9739	−0.0975	0.0690

The parameter ranges of f_{iso}, f_{ic}, and OD are all 0.0~1.0. The POI values are by reference to [19] for WM (normal appearance), GM and CSF, and to [20] for G2~G4 glioma with T2L for T2 hyperintensity on FLAIR images and CEL for Gd-enhanced on T1WIs.

4   Discussion

Overall, the results align with established findings in the field of dMRI parameter estimation. For example, numerical analysis of the DKI model revealed that the diffusional kurtosis parameter exhibits a shorter arc length L and a smaller curvature radius R compared to the diffusion coefficient. This suggests that the estimation of the former is inherently more challenging than that of the latter, a conclusion further supported by the three-dimensional visualization presented in Fig. 3. The results in the NODDI model also imply that OD estimation is harder than other parameters due to the shorter L and the smaller R. Also, new findings were obtained, such as flat arc shape of f_{iso}, and high dependency between f_{ic} and f_{iso}. Thus, the proposed metrics can provide new properties in parameter estimation, and these new findings offer novel perspectives for interpreting results derived from the analysis of real clinical data.

The analysis of these metrics across various tissue types yielded significant insights. For example, each category of glioma [19] shows different property for NODDI parameters, so that classification difficulty for the grades of G2, G3 and G4 can be different depending on the parameter value. It leads to different difficulty between G2-G3 classification and G3-G4 classification. Similarly, when we distinguish tissue type or subtype with thresholding of dMRI parameter values, its reliability can be judged based on these difficulties as the local parameter characteristics. Therefore, through the preliminary results of this study, the simple metrics could provide new standards for reliability of dMRI parameter estimations under specific measurement settings, which are critical in applications such as diagnosis for lesion grading.

While raising awareness regarding the interpretation of dMRI parameters is one of the objectives of this study, the primary aim lies in enhancing the robustness of parameter estimation, which constitutes the core focus of our research. In particular, the proposed metrics are expected to provide substantial benefits to ML-based parameter estimation frameworks [21]. The ML-based dMRI parameter estimation is a regression problem of direct mapping of signal values $\mathbf{s}$ to estimated parameter $\mathbf{p}$ different from the previous fitting approach based on numerical search, and training dataset is the most important factor. A recent study revealed the importance of training data distribution [22,23], which can make significant influence on estimation results. The metrics introduced in this study can give a guideline for adaptive collection of training data. For example, when parameter estimation difficulty at the target POI is high, the quantity of training data around the POI is recommended to be increased. Moreover, such insightful findings regarding training data distribution become particularly impactful when training regressors with synthetic datasets [24–26]. The proposed metrics offer a principled framework for generating synthetic training data that accounts for the varying degrees of difficulty associated with estimating each parameter. Furthermore, the applicability of our approach extends to a wide range of parametric signal models, including relaxometry [27] and diffusion-relaxation models [28,29], where the underlying model equations are more intricate and the challenges in parameter estimation are substantially greater.

In addition to their post-processing benefits for parameter estimation, the metrics proposed in our framework may also offer valuable insights for evaluating imaging protocols. While it is generally true that a greater number of measurements can enhance estimation accuracy, the situation in dMRI is more complex, as the number of MPG directions and the shells also significantly affect estimation difficulty. The metrics introduced in this study may aid in the design of optimal imaging protocols tailored to specific objectives, particularly under practical clinical constraints such as limited acquisition time or suboptimal signal-to-noise ratios. Furthermore, analyzing changes in metric values across different MPG configurations within the same model is essential for validating the effectiveness of our approach. For that purpose, the metrics L and R are corrected with dimensionality factor of $\sqrt{N}$ so that we can compare among different number of measurements.

A clear limitation of the present study is the exclusion of measurement noise, as the focus was placed on the intrinsic properties of dMRI models. As a subsequent step, we aim to extend our investigation by incorporating measurement noise into the evaluation framework, thereby enabling a more practical assessment of parameter estimation difficulty. As illustrated in Figs. 1 and 2, the cumulative effect of measurement noise at a given POI manifests as the distance from the model submanifold in signal space. To achieve this, it is essential to consider not only the magnitude but also the anisotropic nature of the noise associated with each signal. Specifically, the noise can be decomposed into two components: one parallel and the other orthogonal to the submanifold normal, with the former exerting a more direct influence on estimation error. In this context, realistic noise models such as the Rician distribution [30] must be employed for accurate simulation of measurement conditions. For instance, digital phantoms with known ground-truth parameter values and known noise distributions can be utilized to reveal the relationship between our proposed metrics and standard evaluation indices, such as estimation bias and mean squared error.

Our future work, beyond the directions outlined above, can be broadly categorized into two areas: the development of additional metrics and application of our metrics in practical settings. Firstly, the metrics proposed in this study are derived from individual parameter characteristics, including arc length, curvature radius, and tangent vectors. We aim to introduce new metrics capable of capturing more complex interdependencies among parameters, based on the geometric properties of the submanifold. Secondly, our envisioned practical applications of these metrics in clinical data analysis include studies of breast dMRI and brain MRI. The former focuses on establishing a framework for assessing the reliability of lesion subtype classification using parameters from the DKI model. In the latter, we plan to conduct joint parameter analysis across related models-such as DTI, free water imaging (FWI) [31], and NODDI-to clarify their respective advantages and limitations. In particular, comparative evaluation of FWI and NODDI, which share common parameters like free water volume fraction, will be conducted using our proposed metrics. The findings may inform the selection of the most appropriate model for analyzing specific neurological disorders.

5   Summary

In this study, we proposed new metrics for quantifying estimation difficulty in dMRI model parameters, which is based on submanifold geometry in signal space. Preliminary results showed the potential usefulness for judging reliability of estimated parameters in various measurement settings. In addition, impacts on ML-based parameter estimation and imaging protocol evaluation are expected. Further studies are planned to extend and to validate our scheme, particularly with extensive digital phantom studies by incorporating with measurement noise for revealing the relationship between our metrics and noise distribution.

Acknowledgments. This research was partially supported by Japan Society for the Promotion of Science (JSPS) KAKENHI #25K03475.

Disclosure of Interests. The authors have no relevant financial or non-financial interests to disclose and have no competing interests to declare that are relevant to the content of this article.

References

1. Basser, P.J., Mattiello, J., LeBihan, D.: Estimation of the effective self-diffusion tensor from NMR spin echo. J. Magn. Reson. B **103**, 247–254 (1994)
2. Wessels, T., Wessels, C., Ellsiepen, A., et al.: Contribution of diffusion-weighted imaging in determination of stroke etiology. Am. J. Neuroradiol. **27**(1), 35–39 (2006)
3. Wen, H.M., Lam, W.W., Rainer, T., et al.: Multiple acute cerebral infarcts on diffusion-weighted imaging and risk of recurrent stroke. Neurology **63**(7), 1317–19 (2004)
4. Maier, S.E., Sun, Y., Mulkern, R.V.: Diffusion imaging of brain tumors. NMR Biomed. **23**(7), 849–864 (2010)
5. Tanner, J.E., Stejskal, E.O.: Restricted self-diffusion of protons in colloidal systems by the pulsed-gradient, spin-echo method. J. Chem. Phys. **49**, 1768–1777 (1968)
6. Jensen, J.H., Helpern, J.A., Ramani, A., et al.: Diffusional kurtosis imaging: the quantification of non-Gaussian water diffusion by means of magnetic resonance imaging. Magn. Reson. Med. **53**, 1432–1440 (2005)
7. Le Bihan, D., Breton, E., Lallemand, D., et al.: Separation of diffusion and perfusion in intravoxel incoherent motion MR imaging. Radiology **168**(2), 497–505 (1988)
8. Alexander, D.C., Hubbard, P.L., Hall, M.G., et al.: Orientationally invariant indices of axon diameter and density from diffusion MRI. Neuroimage **52**(4), 1374–89 (2010)
9. Zhang, H., Schneider, T., Wheeler-Kingshott, C.A.G., Alexander, D.C.: NODDI: practical in-vivo neurite orientation dispersion and density imaging of the human brain. Neuroimage **61**, 1000–16 (2012)
10. Palombo, M., Ianus, A., Guerreri, M., et al.: SANDI: a compartment-based model for non-invasive apparent soma and neurite imaging by diffusion MRI. Neuroimage **215**, 116835 (2020)
11. Jelescu, I.O., de Skowronski, A., Geffroy, F., et al.: Neurite exchange imaging (NEXI): a minimal model of diffusion in gray matter with inter-compartment water exchange. Neuroimage **256**, 119277 (2022)
12. Pajevic, S., Basser, P.J.: Parametric and non-parametric statistical analysis of DT-MRI data. J. Magn. Reson. **161**(1), 1–14 (2003)
13. Jones, D.K.: Determining and visualizing uncertainty in estimates of fiber orientation from diffusion tensor MRI. Magn. Reson. Med. **49**, 7–12 (2003)
14. Le Bihan, D.: What can we see with IVIM MRI? Neuroimage **187**, 56–67 (2019)
15. Lenglet, C., Campbell, J.S., Descoteaux, M., et al.: Mathematical methods for diffusion MRI processing. Neuroimage **45**(1), S111-22 (2009)
16. Hori, M., Fukunaga, I., Masutani, Y., et al.: Visualizing non-Gaussian diffusion: clinical application of q-space imaging and diffusional kurtosis imaging of the brain and spine. Magn. Reson. Med. Sci. **11**(4), 221–33 (2012)

17. Yin, J., Sun, H., Wang, Z., et al.: Diffusion kurtosis imaging of acute infarction: comparison with routine diffusion and follow-up MR imaging. Radiology **287**(2), 651–57 (2018)
18. Van Essen, D.C., Smith, S.M., Barch, D.M., et al.: The WU-Minn human connectome project: an overview. Neuroimage **80**, 62–79 (2013)
19. Wen, Q., Kelley, D.A., Banerjee, S., et al.: Clinically feasible NODDI characterization of glioma using multiband EPI at 7 T. Neuroimage Clin. **3**(9), 291–99 (2015)
20. Chung A.W., Seunarine K.K., Clark C.A.: NODDI reproducibility and variability with magnetic field strength: a comparison between 1.5 T and 3 T. Hum. Brain Mapp. **37**(12), 4550–65 (2016)
21. Golkov, V., Dosovitskiy, A., Sperl, J.-I., et al.: q-Space deep learning: Twelve-fold shorter and model-free diffusion MRI scans. IEEE Trans. Med. Imaging **35**(5), 1344–51 (2016)
22. Gyori, N.G., Palombo, M., Clark, C.A., et al.: Training data distribution significantly impacts the estimation of tissue microstructure with machine learning. Magn. Reson. Med. **87**(2), 932–47 (2022)
23. Coelho, S., Baete, S.H., Lemberskiy, G., et al.: Reproducibility of the standard model of diffusion in white matter on clinical MRI systems. Neuroimage **257**, 119290 (2022)
24. Ye, C., Cui, Y., Li, X.: q-Space learning with synthesized training data. In: Bonet-Carne, E., Grussu, F., Ning, L., Sepehrband, F., Tax, C.M.W. (eds.) MICCAI 2019. MV, pp. 123–132. Springer, Cham (2019). https://doi.org/10.1007/978-3-030-05831-9_10
25. Masutani Y.: Noise level matching improves robustness of diffusion MRI parameter inference by synthetic q-space learning. In: 16th International Symposium on Biomedical Imaging (ISBI), pp. 139–42. IEEE, Venice, Italy (2019)
26. Valindria V., Palombo M., Chiou E., et al.: Synthetic q-space learning with deep regression networks for prostate cancer characterisation with verdict. In: 18th ISBI, pp.50–54. IEEE, Nice, France (2021)
27. Birk, F., Mahler, L., Steiglechner, J., et al.: Flexible and cost-effective deep learning for accelerated multi-parametric relaxometry using phase-cycled bSSFP. Sci. Rep. **15**(1), 4825 (2025)
28. Martins, J.P.A., Nilsson, M., Lampinen, B., et al.: Neural networks for parameter estimation in microstructural MRI: application to a diffusion-relaxation model of white matter. Neu-roImage **244**, 118601 (2021)
29. Planchuelo-Gómez, Á., Descoteaux, M., Larochelle, H., et al.: Optimisation of quantitative brain diffusion-relaxation MRI acquisition protocols with physics-informed machine learning. Med. Imaging Anal. **94**, 103134 (2024)
30. Daducci A., Ville D.V.D., Thiran J.P., et al.: Sparse regularization for fiber ODF reconstruction: from the suboptimality of l2 and l1 priors to l0. Med. Imaging Anal. **18**, 820–33 (2014)
31. Pasternak, O., Sochen, N., Gur, Y., et al.: Free water elimination and mapping from diffusion MRI. Magn. Reson. Med. **62**(3), 717–30 (2009)

Susceptibility Distortion Correction of Diffusion MRI with a single Phase-Encoding Direction

Sedigheh Dargahi, Sylvain Bouix$^{(\boxtimes)}$, and Christian Desrosiers

École de technologie supérieure, Montreal, QC, Canada
sedigheh.dargahi.1@ens.etsmtl.ca,
{sylvain.bouix,christian.desrosiers}@etsmtl.ca

Abstract. Diffusion MRI (dMRI) is a valuable tool to map brain microstructure and connectivity by analyzing water molecule diffusion in tissue. However, acquiring dMRI data requires to capture multiple 3D brain volumes in a short time, often leading to trade-offs in image quality. One challenging artifact is susceptibility-induced distortion, which introduces significant geometric and intensity deformations. Traditional correction methods, such as topup, rely on having access to blip-up and blip-down image pairs, limiting their applicability to retrospective data acquired with a single phase encoding direction. In this work, we propose a deep learning-based approach to correct susceptibility distortions using only a single acquisition (either blip-up or blip-down), eliminating the need for paired acquisitions. Experimental results show that our method achieves performance comparable to topup, demonstrating its potential as an efficient and practical alternative for susceptibility distortion correction in dMRI.

Keywords: Diffusion MRI · Susceptibility distortions · Deep learning

1 Introduction

Among neuroimaging techniques, diffusion MRI (dMRI) plays a crucial role in understanding the complex connectivity and microstructural features of the brain [1]. The acquisition of dMRI data involves two key considerations. First, special gradient fields are applied during data collection to make the image sensitive to diffusion in a specific direction. Second, to acquire the needed information, many separate 3D images of the brain must be obtained, as each 3D image provides information about diffusion in just one direction. Consequently, to acquire dMRI data in a reasonable amount of time–typically a few minutes–fast imaging sequences such as Echo Planar Imaging (EPI) are used. Unfortunately, these fast acquisitions often lead to image artifacts, which need to be addressed in post-processing. One of the main artifacts, known as *susceptibility distortion*, changes the geometry of the brain along the phase encoding (PE) direction.

M. Chamberland et al. (Eds.): CDMRI 2025, LNCS 16205, pp. 69–80, 2026.
https://doi.org/10.1007/978-3-032-12837-9_7

When dealing with susceptibility-induced distortions, both traditional and deep learning (DL) techniques have been developed. One of the popular strategies is to acquire reversed-phase encoding directions from which a field map can be estimated (the topup tool in FSL) [2]. In recent years, several deep learning-based susceptibility distortion correction techniques [3,4] have emerged to correct this kind of distortion faster and more accurately than topup [5]. In [6], an unsupervised U-Net minimizes the difference between unwarped images at multiple resolutions to accelerate processing. The approach in [7] uses fiber orientation distributions (FODs) derived from dual-phase dMRI and applies a U-Net (DrC-Net) for correction. FOD estimation is computationally intensive, as it requires fitting high-order spherical harmonic models at each voxel to resolve crossing fibers. When applied to millions of voxels in multi-shell diffusion data, this results in substantial computational demands. [8] employs PSF-EPI images as ground truth for training a correction network, yet this data is rarely acquired in clinical practice.

A common challenge of these methods is the dependence on blip-up and blip-down acquisitions, which are not always available. This reliance limits the broader use of advanced distortion correction techniques. Developing a method that works across different scenarios and data types would thus make distortion correction more accessible and practical for both clinical use and research settings. One of the promising DL method [3] addresses this problem by synthesizing an undistorted EPI image from a structural T1-Weighted (T1w) scan and a single-blip diffusion image. The single-blip image and synthetized image are then used as input to topup to estimate a field map. However, training this method relies on having access to a dataset containing undistorted multi-shot diffusion b0 images paired with single-blip data, which are not commonly acquired. Additionally, topup is still needed to estimate the field map.

In this work, we introduce a slice-wise deep-learning method designed to correct susceptibility distortions in dMRI using only *a single phase-encoding direction*, addressing a limitation in current distortion correction techniques. Our contributions can be summarized as follows. First, unlike traditional approaches such as [2], which require paired acquisitions, our method needs only one phase-encoded distorted dMRI image alongside a corresponding structural T1w image. This broadens the practical applicability, particularly for retrospective datasets where dual-phase acquisitions are not available. Second, our model simultaneously predicts both the Voxel Displacement Map (VDM) and the intensity-corrected b0 image in a single forward pass, simplifying the correction workflow. Finally, by integrating these ideas, we reduce processing times from several minutes typically needed by well-known methods such as Synb0 [3] to mere seconds, facilitating large-scale studies and time-sensitive applications. Experimental results demonstrate that our method not only provides correction quality close to that of dual-phase methods like topup, but also surpasses existing single-phase technique in both accuracy and speed.

2   Method

As illustrated in Fig. 1, the proposed model takes as input distorted blip-up or blip-down b0 images[1] as well as T1w images, and outputs the voxel displacement map for correcting the b0 image. The following sections detail the network architecture, loss function and preprocessing pipeline of our proposed method.

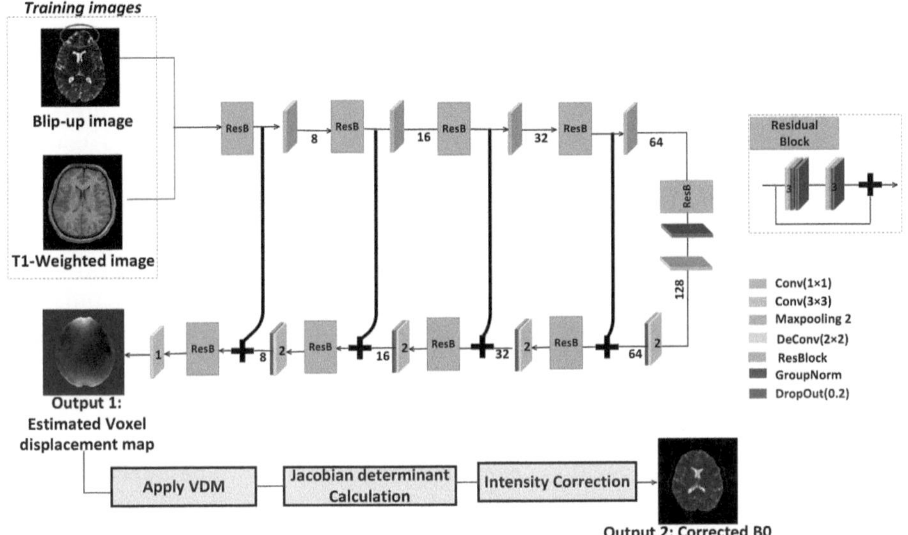

Fig. 1. Architecture of the proposed method.

2.1   Model Architecture

Our proposed model builds on a U-Net architecture, as illustrated in Fig. 1. The encoder consists of sequential residual blocks, each using 3×3 convolutional kernels and skip connections to maintain gradient flow and encourage stable learning. As we progress deeper into the encoder, the number of feature maps increases from 8 to 128, with downsampling performed via max-pooling. The bottleneck features a single residual block with 128 channels, followed by a dropout layer with a rate of 0.2 to help prevent overfitting. The decoder mirrors the encoder's structure, using transposed convolutions to upsample features and gradually reduce the number of channels from 128 back down to 8. Skip connections between corresponding encoder and decoder layers help retain spatial details. The output is generated by a 1×1 convolutional layer, which produces a single-channel VDM.

---

[1] Without loss of generality, we assume in the rest of the paper that blip-up images are given.

To further mitigate overfitting, we made several architectural and regularization choices. Unlike the original U-Net [9], which begins with 64 channels and expands up to 1024 over five downsampling layers, our model is shallower and lighter, starting with just 8 channels and growing to 128 over four levels. To further improve generalization, we introduced dropout (with a probability of 0.2) inside every residual block and after the bottleneck, which is not part of the original U-Net design. Lastly, we apply L1 regularization to penalize large weights, encouraging sparsity in the model parameters. The L1 penalty is added to the total loss with a scaling factor $\lambda_{\mathrm{reg}} = 10^{-5}$.

2.5D Convolutional Approach. While susceptibility distortions only occur along the phase encoding direction within individual 2D slices and are inherently one-dimensional and often localized, our model adopts a 2.5D convolutional strategy to incorporate some 3D context. Instead of using computationally expensive 3D convolutions, we process each slice together with its adjacent neighbors (one slice above and one below) as a 3-channel input. For edge slices (the first and last slices), the nearest slice is duplicated to maintain the three-slice configuration. This approach allows the model to incorporate contextual information from neighboring slices without the need for a full 3D model, striking a good balance between anatomical awareness and computational efficiency.

Distortion correction. The proposed method produces two outputs for each input slice. The first is the predicted voxel displacement map, which estimates spatial distortions along the phase encoding direction in millimeters. The second output is the distortion-corrected b0 image, referred to as $b0^{DL}$. To generate this corrected image, we follow a series of steps based on the procedure described in [10]:

- **Displacement Grid Creation**: Using the VDM, a displacement grid is created, where the VDM values represent displacements along the phase encoding direction. The displacement grid is applied to the first b0 imaging in the dMRI volume.
- **Intensity Correction with the Jacobian Determinant**: To account for intensity variations, the Jacobian determinant of the displacement field is calculated as follows:

$$J_{\mathrm{Field}}(x, y) = 1 + \frac{\partial \mathrm{VDM}(x, y)}{\partial y} \tag{1}$$

  Here y represents the phase-encoding direction. The intensity of the corrected b0 image is then adjusted by multiplying it with the corresponding Jacobian determinant values:

$$\mathrm{b0}^{DL}(x, y) = J_{\mathrm{Field}}(x, y) \cdot \mathrm{b0}_{\mathrm{corrected}}(x, y) \tag{2}$$

- **Final Output**: The resulting image is the corrected $\mathrm{b0}^{DL}$, which is generated by applying this procedure slice by slice, and then stacking the corrected slices to reconstruct the full 3D volume.

2.2   Loss Function

The loss function employed to train the model consists of four terms: L1 loss on the VDMs, L2 loss on the gradients of the VDMs, Structural Similarity Index Measure (SSIM) loss on the corrected b0 images, and Mutual Information (MI) between the T1w and the corrected b0 images. All four losses are computed only within the brain region, defined by a binary mask derived from the T1w image and dilated by 3 pixels to avoid edge artifacts. The choice of these losses is based on the following motivations. We use an L1 loss for the predicted VDMs to reduce the impact of large errors, which frequently occur at the boundaries between different brain tissues. The gradient term is defined as the L2 of the difference between the partial derivatives of the predicted and reference VDMs along the two in-plane axes. It serves as a regularizer that constrains local variations in the deformation field, helping to prevent abrupt changes and encouraging the model to capture structural edges of VDM. To evaluate image-to-image alignment quality, we employ SSIM, as it emphasizes the preservation of structural details, particularly at region boundaries. Finally, we use MI to compare the T1w and b0 images, as it is well-suited for assessing alignment between different imaging modalities. We compute global MI by flattening the masked intensities into a 32-bin joint histogram, then smooth it with a separable Gaussian kernel ($\sigma = 1.0$) to suppress noise and binning artifacts. The negative MI is used as the loss to encourage alignment. The overall loss function is given by

$$\mathcal{L}_{\text{total}} = \lambda_1 \left\| \text{VDM}^{\text{topup}} - \text{VDM}^{\text{DL}} \right\|_1 + \lambda_2 \left\| \nabla \text{VDM}^{\text{topup}} - \nabla \text{VDM}^{\text{DL}} \right\|_2$$
$$+ \lambda_3 \, \text{SSIM}\left(\text{b0}^{\text{topup}}, \text{b0}^{\text{DL}}\right) + \lambda_4 \, \text{MI}\left(\text{T1w}, \text{b0}^{\text{DL}}\right) \tag{3}$$

We place the greatest emphasis on the VDM prediction by setting the L1 loss weight λ_1 to 1, and choose weights of $\lambda_2 = 0.5$, $\lambda_3 = 0.3$, and $\lambda_4 = 0.5$ for the gradient, SSIM, and MI terms, respectively.

2.3   Preprocessing Pipeline

The preprocessing steps are designed to align and prepare the data for input into the model. At first, brain masks are generated for both T1w images and b0 volumes to ensure the focus is on brain tissue and to exclude irrelevant regions. We generate the b0 brain masks using FSL's BET, and the T1w images are masked using FastSurfer's segmentation outputs. Then, the T1w images are rigidly registered to the b0 volumes and resampled to match the dimensions of the b0 images. Finally, three consecutive slices of b0 images are concatenated with the corresponding three slices of T1w images, resulting in a six-channel input with dimensions $6 \times 128 \times 128 \times 80$.

3   Experiments

Dataset. To tackle susceptibility distortions in dMRI, our approach only relies on a single phase-encoding dMRI. We also require a T1w image to provide high-resolution structural information, helping the model guide what an undistorted

brain should look like. The dataset used for training is the National Institute of Mental Health Intramural Healthy Volunteer (NIMH-HV) Dataset [11], which is available on OpenNeuro (https://doi.org/10.18112/openneuro.ds005752.v2.1.0). This dataset includes both blip-up and blip-down acquisitions, allowing us to use dual-phase topup corrections as our ground truth reference for training. The dMRI scans were acquired with the following parameters: echo time (TE) of 60.7 ms, repetition time (TR) of 7.8 s, and voxel dimensions of $1.8125 \times 1.8125 \times 2.0\,\mathrm{mm}^3$. Each scan includes 6 non-diffusion-weighted (b0) volumes and 48 diffusion-weighted directions. This data comprises 125 samples after preprocessing (as not all subjects have DWI). The shape of the data for each subject is $128 \times 128 \times 80 \times 54$. To evaluate how well the model generalizes, we also test it on unseen data of compressed-sensing diffusion spectrum imaging (CS-DSI) [12] which has 20 subjects available on Open-Neuro (https://doi.org/10.18112/openneuro.ds004737.v2.0.0). CS-DSI dMRI scans were acquired with the following parameters: echo time (TE) of 0.09 s, repetition time (TR) of 4.3 s, and voxel dimensions of $1.691 \times 1.691 \times 1.7\,\mathrm{mm}^3$. Each scan includes 7 b0 volumes and 1 diffusion-weighted direction.
We use the following in our approach:

- **Input Data**: The b0 volumes from the DWI dataset are selected as they serve as a reference image free from the diffusion-weighted gradients applied during dMRI scans. These images have a shape of $128 \times 128 \times 80$, corresponding to 80 slices per volume.
- **Silver Standard**: We generate our reference distortion field and corrected b0 image using FSL's topup on paired blip-up/blip-down b0 volumes. We convert the field map in units of Hz to a voxel displacement map in millimeters using the read-out time and the phase-encode voxel size [10]:

$$\mathrm{VDM}^{\mathrm{topup}}(x, y) = \mathrm{FM}(x, y) \; \times \; \mathrm{Read\_Out\_Time} \; \times \; \mathrm{VoxelSize}_y \qquad (4)$$

Finally, to match our network's outputs, we re-apply this VDM (and its Jacobian determinant for intensity modulation) to the original distorted b0, exactly as described in [10]. The resulting silver-standard $(\mathrm{VDM}^{\mathrm{topup}}, \mathrm{b0}^{\mathrm{topup}})$ is used to supervise training of our model.

Orientation Focus and Data Split. Susceptibility distortions occur along the phase encoding direction of the 2D acquisition plane. In most datasets, including the NIMH-HV, the acquisition plane is typically the axial plane and the phase encoding is along the anterior-posterior axis, which is the scenario we assume for our current model.

In our configuration, the NIMH-HV dataset is divided as follows: 75% of the data are assigned for training which would be 93 subjects, 15% of the data for validation which would be 18 subjects, and the remaining 10% for test phase which would be 14 subjects. The splitting is performed randomly to ensure a balanced representation of the dataset. We also applied *on-the-fly augmentations*, where each training slice undergoes, with 50% probability, one of the following transformations: a random integer-valued translation of up to ±5 pixels in both directions; a square crop of variable size (50%–90% of the image) followed by zero-padding back to the original dimensions; additive Gaussian noise ($\sigma = 0.05$) to simulate acquisition variability. In addition, we included horizontal flips and a "mixcut" operation, in which the right half of one subject's slice is spliced with the corresponding left half of another subject's slice to further diversify spatial patterns. These two types of augmentation are well-suited for our application, as susceptibility distortion occurs only along the y-axis. As a result, the silver-standard VDMs of horizontally flipped or half-cut images can be used directly without modification. By combining these five augmentations, we encourage the network to learn distortion-invariant features while preserving anatomical consistency.

Implementation Details. The model is implemented in PyTorch and trained on a Linux system with an NVIDIA RTX A6000 GPU. We use the Adam optimizer with an initial learning rate of 10^{-3}, and apply a scheduler that halves the learning rate if the validation loss does not improve for 5 epochs. To avoid overfitting, early stopping halts training after 30 stagnant epochs. The model is trained for up to 96 epochs with a batch size of 8, total of 62 min of training.

4   Results

4.1   Comparison with State-of-the-Art Methods

We evaluate the performance of our model against Synb0, using topup as the reference on both the NIMH-HV and the external CS-DSI data; the results are reported in Table 1. We chose Synb0 for comparison because, like our method, it works with only a single blip-up or blip-down image, making it a fair comparison. To ensure consistency, we took FM estimated by Synb0 and applied the same steps used for our method and topup, following the procedure in [10], to generate both the VDM and the corrected b0 image. As shown in Table 1, our method outperforms Synb0 in terms of both VDM and b0 Root Mean Squared Error (RMSE). On the NIMH-HV, the VDM RMSE is reduced by about 53%, while the b0 RMSE improves by about 8%. A similar trend holds for the CS-DSI data, where our model reduces the VDM RMSE by roughly one-third and achieves a slight reduction in b0 RMSE. We also compute the mutual information between each corrected b0 image and the T1w image. While topup remains the silver standard with the highest MI, our method boosts MI relative to Synb0 (approximately 0.5% on NIMH-HV, and 6.1% on CS-DSI), indicating improved anatomical alignment, although these improvements are small.

In terms of runtime, Synb0 requires separate steps to correct each volume: almost 15 min to synthesize the undistorted b0 image, followed by more than 6 min to run topup using that synthesized image as input for correction. In contrast, our method performs the entire correction in a single forward pass and completes inference in just a few seconds, making it much faster for large-scale or time-sensitive studies. Overall, these results demonstrate that our deep learning-based correction reduces distortion errors compared to Synb0, even when tested on completely unseen CS-DSI volumes. Additionally, the runtimes improves from tens of minutes to just a few seconds.

Table 1. Comparison of VDM and b0 RMSE for Synb0 and our method with ground truth topup; and Mutual Information (MI) comparison of topup, Synb0 and our method with T1w image on NIMH-HV and CS-DSI datasets. All metrics are averaged across the held-out test subjects and reported as mean (standard deviation).

Dataset	Method	VDM RMSE $\downarrow$	b0 RMSE $\downarrow$	MI $\uparrow$
NIMH-HV	topup	n/a	n/a	0.7620 (0.0785)
	Synb0	2.34 (0.53)	1.91×10^2 (0.348×10^2)	0.7029 (0.1031)
	Ours	1.10 (0.31)	1.76×10^2 (0.339×10^2)	0.7062 (0.0743)
CS-DSI	topup	n/a	n/a	0.5492 (0.0483)
	Synb0	1.95 (0.26)	7.49×10^2 (1.19×10^2)	0.4378 (0.0537)
	Ours	1.31 (0.11)	7.46×10^2 (1.11×10^2)	0.4645 (0.0384)

Figure 2 showcases the results of the proposed method, including the predicted VDMs and corrected b0 images, compared to those generated by topup and Synb0. While topup typically achieves the best anatomical alignment, thanks to its use of both blip-up and blip-down acquisitions, it cannot be applied when only a single phase-encoded image is available. Synb0 often under or overestimates broad distortion patterns. By contrast, our network learns a more accurate displacement map from a single input image. These results suggest that our approach can deliver neartopup quality with a single input image, making it a versatile alternative in data-limited scenarios.

We also compared each method's MI against the T1w image using paired t-test (you can see the results in Fig. 3). Under the paired t-test, topup achieves the highest median MI and outperforms Synb0 as well as our method, whereas the gap between Synb0 and ours does not reach significance. These statistics show that our approach achieves anatomical alignment on par with Synb0 and nearly as good as topup, despite using only one encoding direction.

4.2   Ablation Study

In this section, we evaluate two important design choices we made in building our network: (*i*) the use of a T1w image as input to guide anatomical accuracy and (*ii*) the addition of the gradient of the VDM as a loss term to improve sharpness in VDM reconstruction.

Using T1w. In this experiment, we evaluate how much the T1w image contributes when used both as an additional input and as a term in the loss function. To isolate its effect, we retrain our model using only the b0 image as an input and set the weight of the T1w loss term to zero. Table 2 summarizes the results. As

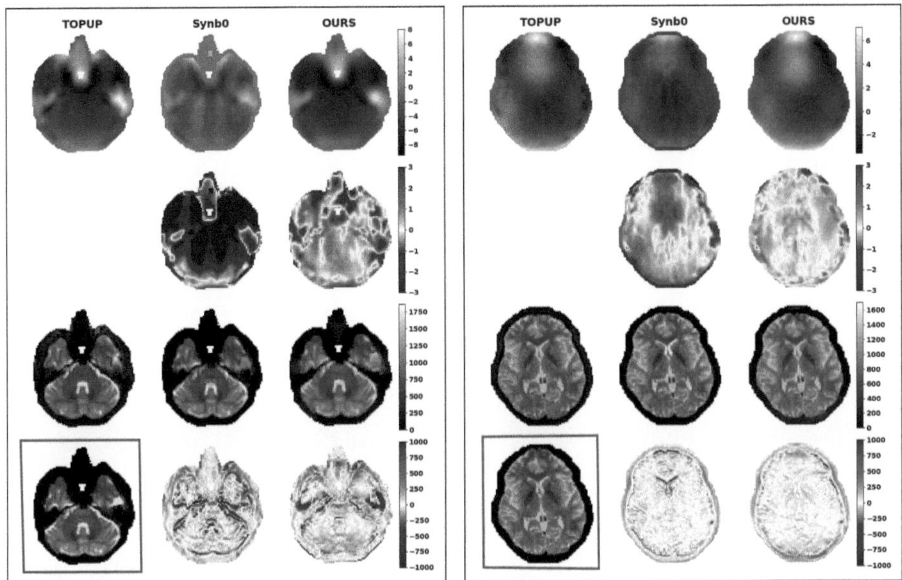

Fig. 2. Comparison of topup, Synb0, and our method for two NIMH-HV test subjects: (left) ON94856 slice 21 and (right) ON95003 slice 36. Rows show: predicted VDMs, VDM differences vs. topup, corrected b0 images, and distorted dMRI (with red box) alongside b0 differences.

can be seen, including the T1w image leads to an improvement across every metric. The VDM RMSE decreases by nearly 26%, the corrected b0 error drops by

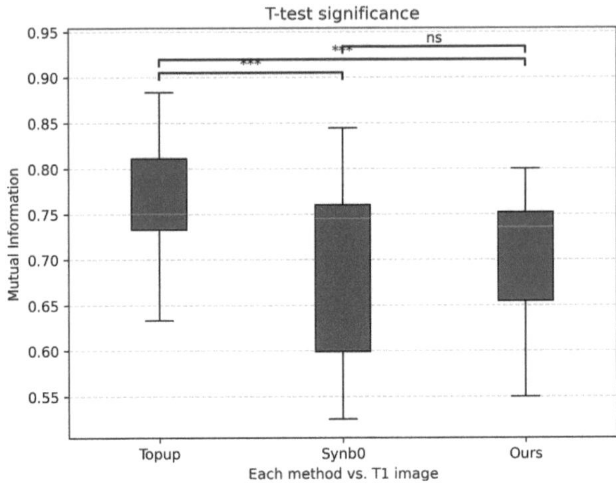

Fig. 3. Each method's MI against the T1-weighted image for paired t-test.

Table 2. Effect of using T1w image and including the VDM gradient loss on performance. All metrics are averaged across the held-out test subjects and reported as mean (standard deviation).

Configuration	VDM RMSE $\downarrow$	b0 RMSE $\downarrow$	MI $\uparrow$
With T1w	1.10 (0.31)	1.76×10^2 (0.339×10^2)	0.7062 (0.0743)
Without T1w	1.48 (0.49)	1.97×10^2 (0.422×10^2)	0.6605 (0.0698)
With gradient loss	1.10 (0.31)	1.76×10^2 (0.339×10^2)	0.7062 (0.0743)
Without gradient loss	1.22 (0.35)	1.80×10^2 (0.344×10^2)	0.7080 (0.0742)

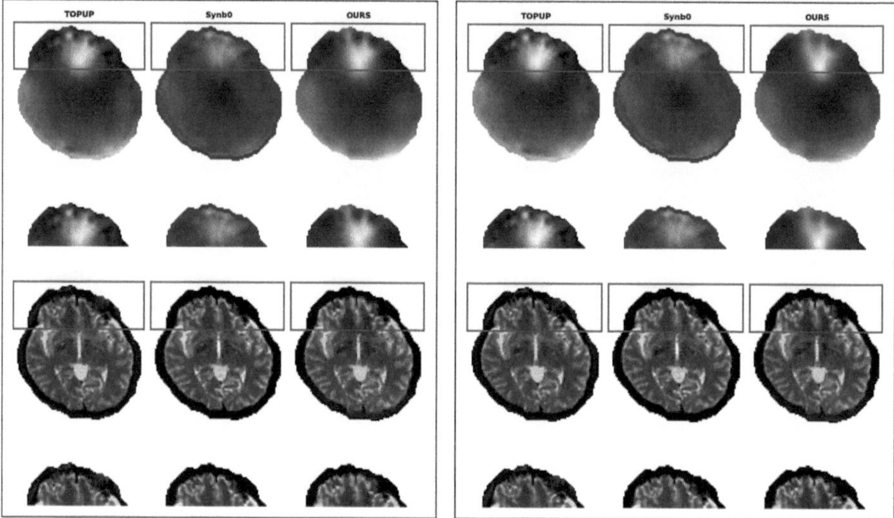

Fig. 4. Visual comparison of topup, Synb0, and our method for NIMH-HV subject ON93426 (slice 36) left image with and right image without the VDM gradient loss. The results indicate minimal visual differences between models trained with or without the gradient loss term, highlighting the network's inherent ability to produce smooth displacement fields.

roughly 11%, and MI improves by about 7%, indicating that the model learns more precise displacement fields when guided by T1w's distortion-free anatomy. This confirms that the T1w image provides valuable anatomical context that improves correction quality.

Using the gradient loss term. Next, we remove the gradient-based term on the predicted VDMs to understand its impact on the final correction. As reported in the bottom half of Table 2, removing the gradient term leads to a modest increase in VDM and b0 RMSE, a slight raise in MI with the T1w image. Both sets of VDMs, whether trained with or without the gradient penalty, remain smoother than the topup reference as shown in Fig. 4, suggesting our network's architecture already favors smooth displacement estimates. Therefore, the extra gradient-loss term delivers only a small numeric gain in RMSE but does not yield any clear boost in anatomical alignment.

4.3 Conclusion

In this work, we introduce a deep learningbased framework for susceptibility distortion correction in diffusion MRI that requires only a single blip-up or blip-down acquisition. By training a 2.5D UNet to jointly predict the VDM and the intensity-corrected b0 image, we demonstrate that it is possible to recover nearly the same geometric and contrast information that topup provides in a faster way, despite never seeing a reverse-phase image. Across both the NIMH-HV dataset and unseen CS-DSI samples, our method is more accurate and significantly faster than Synb0.

Nevertheless, a performance gap remains between our single-input correction and the dual-phase silver standard topup. In future work, we aim to further close this gap by refining our model and extending it to address additional artifacts such as eddy currents and subject motion. We also plan to investigate the model's applicability to other PE directions, and quantify downstream effects for example, FOD coherence, tractography accuracy, and scanrescan reproducibility. Overall, our findings highlight the potential of deep learning as a practical, fast, and versatile alternative to traditional correction methods in diffusion MRI; especially in scenarios where only a single phase-encoding direction is available.

Acknowledgments. This research is supported by NIMH award U24MH124629 (SD, SB) and the Canada Research Chairs Program (SB).

Disclosure of Interests. We do not have any competing interests.

References

1. Jenkinson, M., Beckmann, C.F., Behrens, T.E.J., Woolrich, M.W., Smith, S.M.: Introduction to Neuroimaging Analysis. OUP Oxford (2018)
2. Andersson, J.L.R., Skare, S., Ashburner, J.: How to correct susceptibility distortions in spin-echo echo-planar images: application to diffusion tensor imaging. Neuroimage **20**(2) (2003)
3. Schilling, K.G., et al.: Synthesized bo for diffusion distortion correction (Synbo-DisCo). Magn. Reson. Imaging **64**, 62–70 (2019)
4. Alkilani, Z., Abdallah, A., Çukur, T., Saritas, E.U.: FD-Net: an unsupervised deep forward-distortion model for susceptibility artifact correction in EPI. Magn. Reson. Med. **91**(1), 280–296 (2024)
5. Tax, C.M.W., Bastiani, M., Veraart, J., Garyfallidis, E., Irfanoglu, M.O.: What's new and what's next in diffusion MRI preprocessing. Neuroimage **249**, 118830 (2022). https://doi.org/10.1016/j.neuroimage.2021.118830
6. Zahneisen, B., Baeumler, K., Zaharchuk, G., Fleischmann, D., Zeineh, M.: Deep flow-net for EPI distortion estimation. Neuroimage **217**, 116886 (2020)
7. Qiao, Y., Shi, Y.: Unsupervised deep learning for FOD-based susceptibility distortion correction in diffusion MRI. IEEE Trans. Med. Imaging **41**(5) (2022)

8. Hu, Z., et al.: Distortion correction of single-shot EPI enabled by deep-learning. Neuroimage **221**, 117170 (2020)
9. Ronneberger, O., Fischer, P., Brox, T.: U-Net: convolutional networks for biomedical image segmentation. In: Navab, N., Hornegger, J., Wells, W.M., Frangi, A.F. (eds.) MICCAI 2015. LNCS, vol. 9351, pp. 234–241. Springer, Cham (2015). https://doi.org/10.1007/978-3-319-24574-4_28
10. Liu, S., Xiong, Y., Dai, E., Zhang, J., Guo, H.: Improving distortion correction for isotropic high-resolution 3D diffusion MRI by optimizing Jacobian modulation. Magn. Reson. Med. **86** (2021)
11. Nugent, A.C., et al.: The NIMH intramural healthy volunteer dataset: a comprehensive MEG, MRI, and behavioral resource. Sci. Data **9**, 518 (2022). https://doi.org/10.1038/s41597-022-01623-9
12. Radhakrishnan, H., et al.: CS-DSI. OpenNeuro. [Dataset] (2024). https://doi.org/10.18112/openneuro.ds004737.v2.0.0

Fully Automated Segmentation of Fiber Bundles in Anatomic Tracing Data

Kyriaki-Margarita Bintsi[1]([✉]), Yaël Balbastre[2], Jingjing Wu[1],
Julia F. Lehman[3], Suzanne N. Haber[3,4], and Anastasia Yendiki[1]

[1] Athinoula A. Martinos Center for Biomedical Imaging,Massachusetts General Hospital and Harvard Medical School,Charlestown, MA, USA
`kbintsi@mgh.harvard.edu`
[2] Department of Experimental Psychology,University College London, London, UK
[3] Department of Pharmacology and Physiology, University of Rochester School of Medicine, Rochester, NY, USA
[4] McLean Hospital, Belmont, MA, USA

Abstract. Anatomic tracer studies are critical for validating and improving diffusion MRI (dMRI) tractography. However, large-scale analysis of data from such studies is hampered by the labor-intensive process of annotating fiber bundles manually on histological slides. Existing automated methods often miss sparse bundles or require complex post-processing across consecutive sections, limiting their flexibility and generalizability. We present a streamlined, fully automated framework for fiber bundle segmentation in macaque tracer data, based on a U-Net architecture with large patch sizes, foreground aware sampling, and semi-supervised pre-training. Our approach eliminates common errors such as mislabeling terminals as bundles, improves detection of sparse bundles by over 20% and reduces the False Discovery Rate (FDR) by 40% compared to the state-of-the-art, all while enabling analysis of standalone slices. This new framework will facilitate the automated analysis of anatomic tracing data at a large scale, generating more ground-truth data that can be used to validate and optimize dMRI tractography methods.

Keywords: Anatomic tracing · fiber bundle segmentation · semi-supervised learning

1 Introduction

Diffusion Magnetic Resonance Imaging (dMRI) tractography has emerged as a crucial non-invasive technique for in vivo reconstruction of white matter pathways, playing a vital role in understanding psychiatric and neurological disorders [1,22]. However, its accuracy is limited by the fact that dMRI relies on indirect measurements of axonal orientations based on water diffusion, and that its millimeter scale resolution is much coarser than the size of individual axons [4,17].

© The Author(s), under exclusive license to Springer Nature Switzerland AG 2026
M. Chamberland et al. (Eds.): CDMRI 2025, LNCS 16205, pp. 81–92, 2026.
https://doi.org/10.1007/978-3-032-12837-9_8

In contrast, anatomic tracer studies in non-human primates (NHPs) allow direct visualization of axonal trajectories at the microscale. These studies provide crucial ground-truth data for validating and understanding white matter pathways reconstructed through non-invasive neuroimaging in humans. Comparison between tracer injections and dMRI in the same NHP samples has yielded valuable information on the anatomic accuracy of different dMRI acquisition and analysis methods [13,23].

Microscopy data from brains that have received anatomic tracer injections allow detailed visualization of axonal projections from the injection sites, as they travel through the white matter to reach their terminals. This high-resolution mapping reveals intricate brain connectivity patterns beyond what can be resolved with dMRI tractography, including how the fibers originate, branch into sub-bundles, and take tortuous routes all the way to their terminations [6,13,14]. However, a significant bottleneck in leveraging such data lies in the manual annotation of axon bundles in histological slides, which is extremely time- and labor-intensive. This has restricted the availability of annotated data and, consequently, limited large-scale validation studies of dMRI.

Previous work in automating this annotation has been limited [15,16]. The vast majority of existing axon segmentation methods focus on dense ultra high-resolution images such as those acquired with electron microscopy [10, 18]. These methods are not applicable to images of whole NHP brain sections acquired at micrometer resolution, where the segmentation task is to separate axon bundles that contain tracers from other sources of signal (injection site, terminals, background signal). In this context, work has been mostly limited to images acquired with light-sheet fluorescence microscopy in mice [3,19], where imaging is inherently three-dimensional. Segmentation of tracer data has also been performed in marmoset monkeys, using serial two-photon imaging [21] and serial histology [20]. In both cases, all positively stained pixels were segmented, without differentiating axons from their terminals. Macaques provide a closer homologue to the human brain than marmosets, making them more suitable for translational research [2]. A deep-learning method for segmenting axon bundles in macaque tracer data was proposed in [16]. Although it is a significant first step towards automating this task, this method relies significantly on post-processing to reduce false positives by comparison of predicted bundles across consecutive sections, hence limiting its applicability to single sections. Additionally, the limited training data used in that work affect the generalizability of the model, as seen, e.g., from its limited accuracy in detecting sparse fiber bundles. Thus, it is suitable for computer-aided, rather than fully automated, segmentation.

Here we propose a semi-supervised framework for fiber bundle segmentation in macaque tracer data. Our approach is based on U-Net architectures enhanced with pre-training strategies, and it is designed to operate effectively with limited manual annotations. We evaluate our method in multiple macaque brains with tracer injections in varying sites, demonstrating its ability to generalize across brains and fiber configurations. Our approach outperforms the state-of-the-art, including a 22% improvement for sparse fiber bundles. The code is available on GitHub at: https://github.com/lincbrain/fiber-bundle-segmentation.

2   Methods

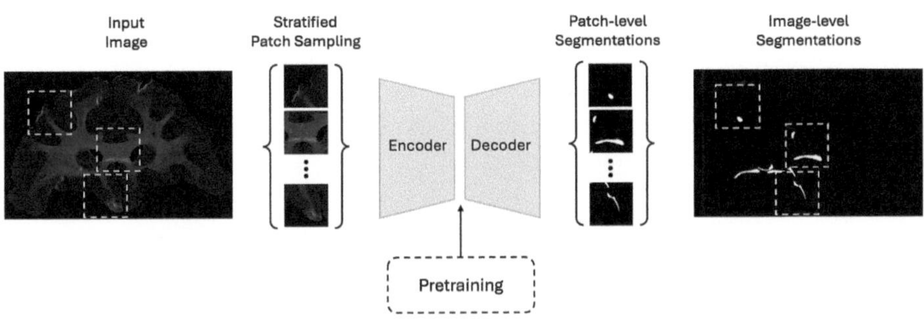

Fig. 1. Proposed pipeline. Patches are extracted from the images using a stratified patch sampling technique that ensures foreground is available to 50% of the patches. These patches are then used to train a U-Net. Patch-level segmentations are combined back to image-level. Pre-training of the U-Net for a reconstruction task is used to leverage the availability of unlabeled images.

An overview of the pipeline can be found in Fig. 1.

2.1   Patch Sampling and Pre-Processing

Due to the large size of the histological images and the sparsity of annotated fiber bundles, we adopt a patch-based training strategy. Each whole-slide image is downsampled (see Sect. 3.1) and divided into smaller patches for model training and inference.

We apply Z-score normalization to stabilize training. During training, we extract 20 random patches of size 1024×1024 pixels from each section. We deploy a stratified patch sampling approach, which ensures that 50% of the sampled patches contain foreground (i.e., fiber bundles), thereby balancing background and foreground regions.

To account for limited labeled data, we use a combination of data augmentation strategies - horizontal and vertical flips and elastic transformations.

2.2   Model Architecture and Training

We employ a 2D U-Net architecture [12] for fiber bundle segmentation. Our configuration for network training involves a combination of Binary Cross Entropy (BCE) and Dice loss.

Additionally, we consider an alternative setup using a combination of Focal Loss [9] and Dice Loss, designed to address class imbalance and enhance overlap with the ground truth.

The total loss function is defined as:

$$\mathcal{L}_{\text{total}} = \mathcal{L}_{\text{BCE}} + \mathcal{L}_{\text{Dice}} \quad \text{or} \quad \mathcal{L}_{\text{total}} = \mathcal{L}_{\text{Focal}} + \mathcal{L}_{\text{Dice}}, \tag{1}$$

depending on the configuration. The BCE loss is given by:

$$\mathcal{L}_{\text{BCE}} = -\frac{1}{N} \sum_{i=1}^{N} \left[g_i \log(p_i) + (1 - g_i) \log(1 - p_i) \right], \tag{2}$$

where p_i and g_i denote the predicted and ground truth probabilities for pixel i, respectively. The Focal Loss is defined as:

$$\mathcal{L}_{\text{Focal}} = -\frac{1}{N} \sum_{i=1}^{N} \alpha_t (1 - p_t)^\gamma \log(p_t), \tag{3}$$

where p_t is the predicted probability for the true class, and α_t, γ are hyperparameters used to balance class weights and focus training on hard examples. The Dice Loss is:

$$\mathcal{L}_{\text{Dice}} = 1 - \frac{2 \sum_i p_i g_i}{\sum_i p_i + \sum_i g_i + \epsilon}, \tag{4}$$

with ϵ added to prevent division by zero.

2.3 Inference and Postprocessing

At inference time, the model processes each image using a sliding window approach with a stride of 25% of the patch size. The resulting probability maps from overlapping patches are averaged to form a final prediction map. Postprocessing steps include Gaussian smoothing, mirroring, and removal of very small connected components that likely represent noise.

2.4 Self-Supervised Pre-Training

While manually labeled sections are scarce, unlabeled sections are plentiful. To leverage the latter, we investigate whether self-supervised pre-training improves downstream segmentation performance. Specifically, we pre-train the U-Net on an image reconstruction task. The network is trained to reconstruct an input histological patch from a compressed latent representation, encouraging the encoder to learn meaningful structural features of tracer data.

We use Mean Squared Error (MSE) as the reconstruction loss:

$$\mathcal{L}_{\text{MSE}} = \frac{1}{N} \sum_{i=1}^{N} (x_i - \hat{x}_i)^2, \tag{5}$$

where x_i and $\hat{x}_i$ are the pixel values of the input and reconstructed image, respectively, and N is the total number of pixels in a patch.

The learned weights are then used to initialize the segmentation network, which is subsequently fine-tuned using labeled data.

3   Experiments

3.1   Datasets

We used high-resolution coronal histological sections of macaque brains with injections of bidirectional tracers at different cortical sites. In total, data from $N = 20$ macaques were included, with injection sites at distinct anatomical areas, resulting in a diverse set of axonal trajectories and fiber configurations.

The histological sections had a thickness of 50 µm, and were digitized with an in-plane resolution of 0.4 µm. To reduce redundancy and processing load while maintaining anatomical continuity, every eighth section was stained to visualize a specific tracer, resulting in an effective inter-slice gap of 400 µm. This sampling strategy follows previous tracer studies in non-human primates [5,8].

Due to the labor-intensive nature of manual annotations, expert-labeled ground truth is available for a limited subset of the data: five complete macaque brains (M1-M5). All annotations were performed by an expert neuroanatomist and include segmentation of three classes of fiber bundles: dense, moderate, and sparse. A fiber bundle is defined here as a group of axons that travel in close proximity to each other, from the injection site toward one or more terminal fields.

Because the original 2D histological images were extremely large, we downsampled all images by a factor of 4 prior to training and evaluation, yielding a resolution suitable for processing while preserving key anatomical features.

In total, we collected 898 histological sections (labeled and unlabeled) from macaques M1M20, of which 165 sections had manually annotated fiber bundles. For model training and validation, we used the complete data set of macaque M1 and the anterior and posterior halves of sections from macaques M2 and M3, respectively. For model testing, we used the left-out halves of M2 and M3 sections, and the complete datasets of M4 and M5, allowing us to evaluate the generalization of the model to unseen brains and fiber trajectories.

3.2   Evaluation Metrics

We follow the evaluation protocol from [16] to allow for a direct comparison of performance.

True positive rate; TPR (Sensitivity). We quantify sensitivity by the TPR, which measures the proportion of fiber bundles in the ground truth that are correctly detected by the model. We report sensitivity separately for each fiber bundle class: dense, moderate, and sparse. Note that our model does not discriminate between these classes during training or inference, but evaluating performance by class is informative, as will be shown below. The TPR for each class is computed as:

$$\mathrm{TPR}_{\mathrm{class}} = \frac{\mathrm{TP}_{\mathrm{class}}}{\mathrm{TP}_{\mathrm{class}} + \mathrm{FN}_{\mathrm{class}}}, \tag{6}$$

where $\mathrm{TP}_{\mathrm{class}}$ denotes the number of ground truth bundles of a given class that are successfully matched by a predicted bundle, and $\mathrm{FN}_{\mathrm{class}}$ are ground truth bundles of that class with no corresponding prediction. Bundle-wise matching is determined via connected component analysis.

Average number of true and false positives per section (TP_{avg}, FP_{avg}). These metrics represent the average number of predicted fiber bundles per test section that correctly (TP) or incorrectly (FP) overlap with ground truth annotations. A predicted bundle is counted as a true positive if it overlaps with any ground truth bundle, and as a false positive otherwise. The average is computed by dividing the total TP and FP counts by the number of test sections.

False discovery rate (FDR). The FDR quantifies the proportion of incorrect positive predictions among all positive predictions made by the model, with a lower FDR indicating fewer false positives. FDR is given by:

$$\text{FDR} = \frac{\text{FP}}{\text{TP} + \text{FP}}, \tag{7}$$

where TP and FP are computed as described above using component-wise matching between predictions and ground truth.

3.3   Implementation Details

We employ a flexible 2D U-Net architecture [12]. The network consists of an encoder and decoder with skip connections. The number of feature maps doubles after each downsampling block in the encoder, starting from a base of 32 and capped at 512. Specifically, we have nine resolution levels in total. The decoder performs upconvolution followed by concatenation with the corresponding encoder output and a double convolution block. ReLU is used as the activation function in all convolutional blocks. The network is trained with the Adam optimizer [7] and a base learning rate of 10^{-4} for 1000 epochs. To maximize robustness and minimize variance, we performed 5-fold cross-validation. The final prediction for each patch was obtained by averaging the scores from all 5 models. During inference, we applied a grid sampling strategy with overlapping patches (using a stride of 0.25 of the patch size) and then blended overlapping regions to produce the final segmentation. The pipeline was implemented in PyTorch [11] and trained on a Titan RTX GPU.

4   Results

To provide a baseline for comparison, we first evaluated the state-of-the-art [16] on our test set. We then trained four variations of our model: 1) using the exact same training dataset as in [16], which we refer to as D_{small}; 2) using the larger training set described in Sect. 3.1, which we refer to as D_{large}, but including only dense and moderate bundles as was done in [16]; 3) using the larger training set and including dense, moderate, and sparse bundles, which we refer to as $D_{\text{large+sparse}}$; and 4) repeating (3) with the use of pre-training. The test set consists of the annotated sections from brains M2 and M3 that were

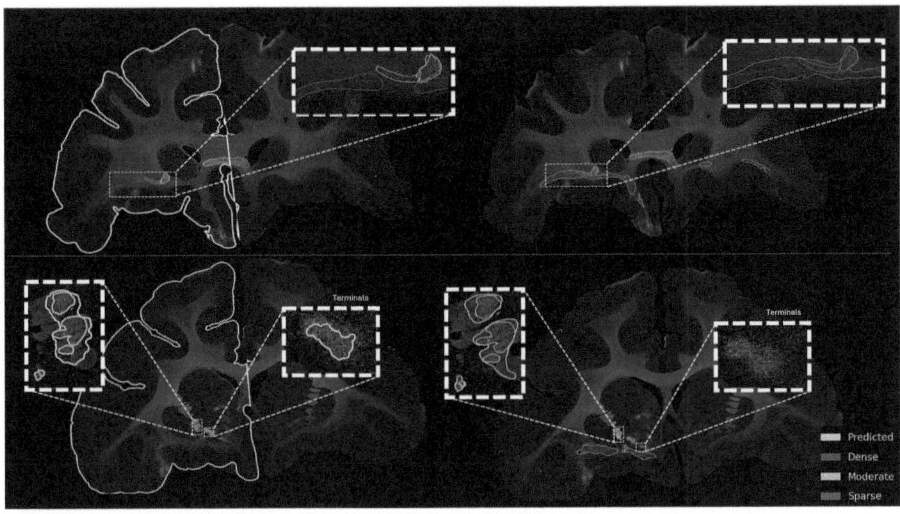

Fig. 2. Visual comparison between **the state-of-the-art method** [16] **(left)** and **our approach (right)** on two histological sections. Predicted segmentations are shown in yellow. Ground truth annotations indicate dense bundles in green, moderate bundles in cyan, and sparse bundles in red. Our approach is able to detect sparse bundles that the baseline misses **(top row)**, while also correctly separating terminals from fiber bundle areas **(bottom row)**. Note that we have ground truth annotations only inside the white outline (ipsilateral hemisphere), hence predictions made outside this outline are not included in the evaluation metrics.

not used during training, as well as all annotated sections from two additional brains, M4 and M5. The results are summarized in Table 1.

Our pipeline performed best when leveraging pre-training and the $D_{\text{large+sparse}}$ dataset. It demonstrated strong performance across all bundles, yielding $\text{TPR}_{\text{dense}} = 0.98$, $\text{TPR}_{\text{moderate}} = 0.94$, and $\text{TPR}_{\text{sparse}} = 0.71$, while increasing true positives ($\text{TP}_{\text{avg}} = 3.11$) and reducing low FP_{avg} at 1.13 and FDR at 0.19. Importantly, it performed considerably better than the baseline [16] ($\text{TPR}_{\text{sparse}}$ at 0.49 and FDR at 0.63).

Qualitative comparisons between our best configuration and the baseline [16] can be found in Fig. 2. The baseline method detects dense bundles but misses several moderate and most sparse ones (Fig. 2 **top row**). In contrast, our method correctly identifies bundles across all density levels. Additionally, while the baseline predicts some moderate bundles, it largely misses sparse ones and erroneously labels terminals as fiber areas (Fig. 2 **bottom row**). Our model resolves both issues, producing more complete and accurate segmentations. Note here that manual annotations were available only within the brain outlines shown in the figures, which typically included only the ipsilateral hemisphere of the injection site. As we did not have ground truth labels outside that outline, we excluded any predictions outside the outline when computing evaluation metrics, for both our models and the baseline model (seen on the left of Fig. 2).

Table 1. Performance of the proposed approach, with the state-of-the-art [16] for fiber bundle segmentation from anatomic tracing data acting as a baseline for comparison. Explanations of the datasets and the metrics can be found in Sect. 3.1 and Sect. 3.2 respectively.

Model	Training dataset	TPR $\uparrow$ dense/moderate/sparse	TP_{avg} $\uparrow$	FP_{avg} $\downarrow$	FDR $\downarrow$
Baseline [16]	D_{small}	0.93/0.80/0.49	1.00	3.07	0.63
Ours (1)	D_{small}	0.92/0.87/0.60	1.82	1.08	0.24
Ours (2)	D_{large}	0.97/0.85/0.66	2.54	0.66	0.16
Ours (3)	$D_{\text{large+sparse}}$	0.98/0.94/0.74	2.81	1.37	0.28
Ours+pre-train (4)	$D_{\text{large+sparse}}$	0.98/0.94/0.71	3.11	1.13	0.19

It is important to note, however, that predictions outside the outline are not necessarily false positives, as we do expect the injection sites to project to the contralateral hemisphere.

4.1   Ablation Studies

Expansion of the training set. This comparison highlights how additional manually annotated training data influence performance. Comparing the U-Net trained on D_{small} (Table 1:(1)), that is, the same training data distribution as the baseline [16], we notice that our model improves performance, with an almost 3x reduction in FP_{avg} from 3.07 to only 1.08. Leveraging more data with D_{large} (Table 1:(2)), even without including sparse bundles, already leads to improvement - yielding TPR_{dense} of 0.97 (vs. 0.92) and TPR_{sparse} of 0.66 (vs. 0.60) - while increasing TP_{avg} from 1.82 to 2.54 and reducing FDR from 0.24 to 0.16.

Inclusion of sparse bundles during training. Here we observe the effects of adding sparse bundles to the training set (Table 1:(3)). Our network (without pre-training) performs better at detecting sparse bundles - TPR_{sparse} jumped from 0.66 to 0.74 - suggesting that including them in the training set is crucial for generalizability.

Pre-training. Our results indicate that pre-training (Table 1:(4)) leads to improved model precision, as seen in the lower FDR (0.19 from 0.3), and increases the average number of true positives. However, this comes at the cost of a a slightly reduced sensitivity for sparse bundles to TPR_{sparse} of 0.71 (vs. 0.74). This suggests that reconstruction pretraining may instill a conservative bias in the model's feature representation, making it less responsive to weak foreground signals even after fine-tuning.

Loss functions. To account for class imbalance, we experimented with Focal+Dice loss instead of the traditional BCE+Dice loss under both pretrained and non-pretrained settings. Without pretraining, focal loss improved the true positive average (TPavg: 2.81 vs. 2.65), particularly enhancing recall in sparse fiber bundles. However, this also led to a slightly elevated false discovery rate

(FDR: 0.28 vs. 0.26). When pretraining was applied, focal loss continued to slightly improve TP_{avg} while achieving a lower FDR (0.19 vs. 0.21), indicating that pretraining mitigates the instability often associated with focal loss and leads to better precision-recall tradeoffs overall. We attribute the improved performance of focal loss to its ability to down-weight well-classified (easy) negatives, allowing the model to focus on harder, underrepresented positive examples - a property particularly beneficial in the context of sparse or imbalanced fiber bundle distributions.

5   Discussion

Fiber bundle segmentation from anatomic tracing data is challenging due to the scarcity of manually labeled ground truth. Our work achieves significant performance improvements, taking an important step toward fully automated segmentation and enabling more effective use of tracer data to validate and optimize dMRI tractography.

Our main contribution is to demonstrate that a simplified architecture, using large patch sizes, foreground-aware sampling, and inclusion of sparse bundles during training can outperform a previous, more complex model that relied on temporal ensembling and contextual information from consecutive sections [16]. Our method does not require information from neighboring sections, and can thus work even on standalone sections from new datasets. While individual metric differences may appear subtle, the combined improvements-such as a lower FDR alongside a higher TPR for sparse bundles-reflect a clearer and more consistent enhancement in segmentation performance. By reducing architectural complexity while improving accuracy across all evaluation metrics, we establish a new, strong baseline for future work.

A crucial advancement is our method's ability to accurately detect fiber bundles across the full spectrum of density, including sparse bundles that were previously missed. Additionally, our approach corrects prior mislabeling of terminals as bundles (see Fig. 2), resulting in more precise connectivity mapping. This performance improvement is essential for minimizing the need for manual intervention and moving closer to fully automated segmentation. This will facilitate the processing of data from anatomic tracer studies, towards the ultimate goal of building more complete models of brain circuitry and expanding the availability of ground-truth data to validate dMRI findings.

Although pre-training improves precision, it appears to slightly reduce model sensitivity, particularly in detecting sparse bundles. We hypothesize that this is due to a conservative prediction bias introduced during pre-training, which persists even with full fine-tuning. In future work, we plan to address this limitation by incorporating synthetic training data to increase the diversity and frequency of sparse bundle examples that we present to the network. Additionally, we will explore transformer-based models and masked autoencoders as an alternative pre-training strategy that may encourage more informative and task-relevant feature representations compared to standard image reconstruction. To provide a more comprehensive evaluation of model performance, we aim to include additional object- and pixel-level metrics (e.g., Dice coefficient, IoU, detection rate) in future work. These will help characterize model behavior more fully and facilitate better comparisons across methods. We also recognize the importance of reporting variance across runs to assess robustness, and we plan to incorporate such estimates in subsequent studies. Finally, we plan to extend our model to 3D, so that we can apply it to volumetric imaging data from light-sheet fluorescence microscopy.

6 Conclusions

In this work, we present a framework for automated segmentation of fiber bundles in macaque tracer data that surpasses the state-of-the-art in both accuracy and robustness. Specifically, our framework improves segmentation of sparse bundles and allows single-section analysis. By leveraging simple yet effective architectural and sampling strategies, our approach resolves key limitations of prior work-substantially reducing false positives without relying on complex post-processing or contextual information from neighboring sections. This new baseline will enable broader, more scalable extraction of ground-truth data to validate non-invasive imaging of brain connectivity, and will, more generally, support the transition to fully digitized anatomy studies.

Acknowledgments. This work was supported by the center for Large-scale Imaging of Neural Circuits (LINC), an NIH BRAIN Initiative Connectivity across Scales (CONNECTS) comprehensive center (UM1-NS132358). Additional support was provided by the National Institute for Mental Health (R01-MH045573, P50-MH106435) and the National Institute for Neurological Disorders and Stroke (R01-NS119911, R01-NS127353).

Disclosure of Interests. The authors have no competing interests to declare that are relevant to the content of this article.

References

1. Catani, M.: Diffusion tensor magnetic resonance imaging tractography in cognitive disorders. Curr. Opin. Neurol. **19**(6), 599–606 (2006)
2. Chatterjee, H.J., Ho, S.Y., Barnes, I., Groves, C.: Estimating the phylogeny and divergence times of primates using a supermatrix approach. BMC Evol. Biol. **9**, 1–19 (2009)
3. Friedmann, D., et al.: Mapping mesoscale axonal projections in the mouse brain using a 3D convolutional network. Proc. Natl. Acad. Sci. **117**(20), 11068–11075 (2020)
4. Grisot, G., Haber, S.N., Yendiki, A.: Diffusion MRI and anatomic tracing in the same brain reveal common failure modes of tractography. Neuroimage **239**, 118300 (2021)
5. Haynes, W.I., Haber, S.N.: The organization of prefrontal-subthalamic inputs in primates provides an anatomical substrate for both functional specificity and integration: implications for basal ganglia models and deep brain stimulation. J. Neurosci. **33**(11), 4804–4814 (2013)

6. Jbabdi, S., Lehman, J.F., Haber, S.N., Behrens, T.E.: Human and monkey ventral prefrontal fibers use the same organizational principles to reach their targets: tracing versus tractography. J. Neurosci. **33**(7), 3190–3201 (2013)
7. Kingma, D.P., Ba, J.: Adam: a method for stochastic optimization. arXiv preprint arXiv:1412.6980 (2014)
8. Lehman, J.F., Greenberg, B.D., McIntyre, C.C., Rasmussen, S.A., Haber, S.N.: Rules ventral prefrontal cortical axons use to reach their targets: implications for diffusion tensor imaging tractography and deep brain stimulation for psychiatric illness. J. Neurosci. **31**(28), 10392–10402 (2011)
9. Lin, T.Y., Goyal, P., Girshick, R., He, K., Dollár, P.: Focal loss for dense object detection. In: Proceedings of the IEEE International Conference on Computer Vision, pp. 2980–2988 (2017)
10. Naito, T., Nagashima, Y., Taira, K., Uchio, N., Tsuji, S., Shimizu, J.: Identification and segmentation of myelinated nerve fibers in a cross-sectional optical microscopic image using a deep learning model. J. Neurosci. Methods **291**, 141–149 (2017)
11. Paszke, A.: Pytorch: an imperative style, high-performance deep learning library. arXiv preprint arXiv:1912.01703 (2019)
12. Ronneberger, O., Fischer, P., Brox, T.: U-Net: convolutional networks for biomedical image segmentation. In: Navab, N., Hornegger, J., Wells, W.M., Frangi, A.F. (eds.) MICCAI 2015. LNCS, vol. 9351, pp. 234–241. Springer, Cham (2015). https://doi.org/10.1007/978-3-319-24574-4_28
13. Safadi, Z., et al.: Functional segmentation of the anterior limb of the internal capsule: linking white matter abnormalities to specific connections. J. Neurosci. **38**(8), 2106–2117 (2018)
14. Schilling, K.G., et al.: Limits to anatomical accuracy of diffusion tractography using modern approaches. Neuroimage **185**, 1–11 (2019)
15. Sundaresan, V., Lehman, J.F., Fitzgibbon, S., Jbabdi, S., Haber, S.N., Yendiki, A.: Constrained self-supervised method with temporal ensembling for fiber bundle detection on anatomic tracing data. In: International Workshop on Medical Optical Imaging and Virtual Microscopy Image Analysis, pp. 115–125. Springer (2022)
16. Sundaresan, V., Lehman, J.F., Maffei, C., Haber, S.N., Yendiki, A.: Self-supervised segmentation and characterization of fiber bundles in anatomic tracing data. Imaging Neurosci. **3**, imag_a_00514 (2025)
17. Thomas, C., et al.: Anatomical accuracy of brain connections derived from diffusion MRI tractography is inherently limited. Proc. Natl. Acad. Sci. **111**(46), 16574–16579 (2014)
18. Wei, D., et al.: AxonEM Dataset: 3D axon instance segmentation of brain cortical regions. In: de Bruijne, M., Cattin, P.C., Cotin, S., Padoy, N., Speidel, S., Zheng, Y., Essert, C. (eds.) MICCAI 2021. LNCS, vol. 12901, pp. 175–185. Springer, Cham (2021). https://doi.org/10.1007/978-3-030-87193-2_17
19. Winnubst, J., et al.: Reconstruction of 1,000 projection neurons reveals new cell types and organization of long-range connectivity in the mouse brain. Cell **179**(1), 268–281 (2019)
20. Woodward, A., et al.: The nanozoomer artificial intelligence connectomics pipeline for tracer injection studies of the marmoset brain. Brain Struct. Funct. **225**, 1225–1243 (2020)
21. Yan, M., et al.: Mapping brain-wide excitatory projectome of primate prefrontal cortex at submicron resolution and comparison with diffusion tractography. Elife **11**, e72534 (2022)

22. Yang, J.Y.M., Yeh, C.H., Poupon, C., Calamante, F.: Diffusion MRI tractography for neurosurgery: the basics, current state, technical reliability and challenges. Phys. Med. Biol. **66**(15), 15TR01 (2021)
23. Yendiki, A., Aggarwal, M., Axer, M., Howard, A.F., van Walsum, A.V.C., Haber, S.N.: Post mortem mapping of connectional anatomy for the validation of diffusion MRI. Neuroimage **256**, 119146 (2022)

Author Index

MIX
Papier aus verantwortungsvollen Quellen
Paper from responsible sources
FSC® C105338

If you have any concerns about our products,
you can contact us on
ProductSafety@springernature.com

In case Publisher is established outside the EU,
the EU authorized representative is:
Springer Nature Customer Service Center GmbH
Europaplatz 3, 69115 Heidelberg, Germany

Printed by Libri Plureos GmbH
in Hamburg, Germany